Best Easy Day Hikes
Adirondacks

Help Us Keep This Guide Up to Date

Every effort has been made by the author and editors to make this guide as accurate and useful as possible. However, many things can change after a guide is published—trails are rerouted, regulations change, facilities come under new management, etc.

We would love to hear from you concerning your experiences with this guide and how you feel it could be improved and kept up to date. While we may not be able to respond to all comments and suggestions, we'll take them to heart and we'll also make certain to share them with the author. Please send your comments and suggestions to the following address:

FalconGuides
Reader Response/Editorial Department
246 Goose Lane, Suite 200
Guilford, CT 06437

Or you may e-mail us at:

editorial@Falcon.com

Thanks for your input, and happy trails!

Best Easy Day Hikes Series

Best Easy Day Hikes
Adirondacks

Second Edition

Lisa Densmore Ballard

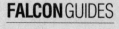

FALCONGUIDES

GUILFORD, CONNECTICUT

To Charles Everitt (1935–2010) who talked me into writing my first book in 1999 and signed me up for the first edition of this one. I hope your outdoor pursuits in heaven are as adventurous as those you had on earth.

FALCONGUIDES®

An imprint of Globe Pequot
Falcon and FalconGuides are registered trademarks and Make Adventure Your Story is a trademark of Rowman & Littlefield.

Distributed by NATIONAL BOOK NETWORK
Copyright © 2017 by Rowman & Littlefield

All rights reserved. No part of this book may be reproduced in any form or by any electronic or mechanical means, including information storage and retrieval systems, without written permission from the publisher, except by a reviewer who may quote passages in a review.

Maps by Design Maps Inc. © Rowman & Littlefield

British Library Cataloguing in Publication Information Available

Library of Congress Cataloging-in-Publication Data

Names: Ballard, Lisa Densmore, author.
Title: Best easy day hikes : Adirondacks / Lisa Densmore Ballard.
Description: Second edition. | Guilford, Connecticut : FalconGuides, 2017. |
  Series: Best Easy Day Hikes Series | Description based on print version
  record and CIP data provided by publisher; resource not viewed.
Identifiers: LCCN 2017003865 (print) | LCCN 2017013645 (ebook) |
  ISBN 9781493024476 (pbk.) | ISBN 9781493024483 (e-book)
Subjects: LCSH: Hiking–New York (State)–Adirondack Mountains–Guidebooks. |
  Trails–New York (State)–Adirondack Mountains–Guidebooks. | Adirondack
  Mountains (N.Y.)–Guidebooks.
Classification: LCC GV199.42.N652 (ebook) | LCC GV199.42.N652 A354 2017
  (print) | DDC 796.5109747/5–dc23
LC record available at https://lccn.loc.gov/2017003865

♾™ The paper used in this publication meets the minimum requirements of American National Standard for Information Sciences—Permanence of Paper for Printed Library Materials, ANSI/NISO Z39.48-1992.

Printed in the United States of America

Contents

The Hikes

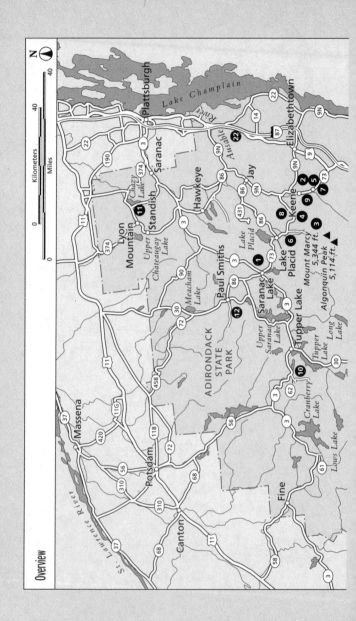

Overview

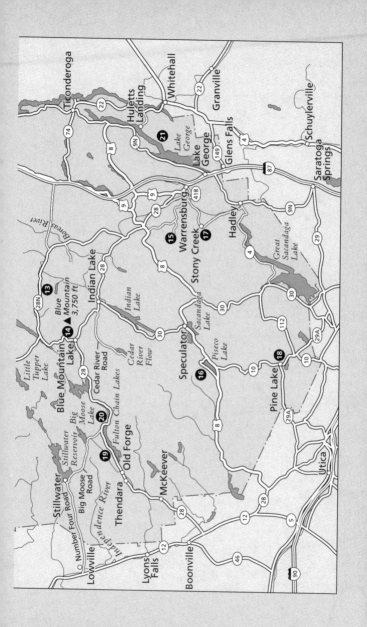

Acknowledgments

I am often asked to name my favorite hikes in the Adirondacks. My favorites are not due to the nuances of the trail or the views—they are exceptional because of the friends and family who accompanied me on the trail: my husband, Jack Ballard; my son, Parker Densmore; my stepdaughter, Zoe Ballard; my brother Wayne Feinberg; and my friends, Peggy Shinn and her daughter, Samantha, Lyndon and Ilyse Tretter, Deborah Hannam and John Donovan, all of whom hiked with me while I was updating this book. Thank you for exploring the Adirondacks with me.

I also owe my sincerest gratitude to Peter Sachs at Lowa. Thank you for your sense of humor and for keeping my feet happy day after day on the trail.

And last but certainly not least, I would like to thank the New York State Department of Environmental Conservation, the Adirondack Mountain Club, the Adirondack Trail Improvement Society and the Adirondack Mountain Reserve for their maintenance of the many paths I followed. With over 2,300 miles of trails in the Adirondack Park, it's a mammoth task, but you help make the Adirondacks a special place to visit.

Introduction

The Adirondack Park is a hiker's nirvana. While known as a mountainous area, the Adirondacks also boast a myriad of paths to lakes and ponds, waterfalls, and rivers. At over six million acres, this state park is larger than Yellowstone, Yosemite, and Glacier National Parks combined. Though a patchwork of public land (48 percent) and private land (52 percent), most of the hiking trails lie within the designated wilderness or wild forest areas of the park. The twenty-two hikes in this book are spread throughout the Adirondacks. No matter where you are in the park, you'll find the best and easiest hikes nearby.

And as for mountaintops, forty-six of them in the Adirondack Park are over 4,000 feet tall. Becoming an "Adirondack 46-er" requires bagging all of these peaks. It's a challenging quest, as twenty of the peaks are extremely remote, even by Adirondack standards, and trail-less, though unofficial "herd paths" now lead to all of the trail-less summits. But there is one that qualifies as a "best easy day hike"—Cascade Mountain, which is described in this book.

Of course, rating a hike "best" and "easiest" is subjective, though in this case, not haphazard. The routes in this book are generally under 6 miles long and promise a big reward for relatively modest effort. You'll certainly find eye-popping views, as well as water, wildlife, unique geologic formations, and interesting plant-life. I discovered these routes while working on the first edition of my larger book, *Hiking the Adirondacks* (FalconGuides, 2010). For more ambitious hikes, plus much more information on and photos of the Adirondack Park, consider adding *Hiking the Adirondacks* to your guidebook collection. In the meantime, this book cherry-picks the best easy hikes in the park for you. Enjoy the trails!

Seasons and Weather

The Adirondack Park has four distinct seasons, though they are not evenly spaced throughout the year. During the short summer—July and August—temperatures can hit the 90s on occasion but the average temperature is a hiker-friendly 68 degrees Fahrenheit. It's also perfect bug-hatching weather. The black flies can be relentless from early June through mid-July, then the mosquitoes take over, especially around streams, beaver ponds, and lakeshores. Don't leave the car without bug repellent.

Fall comes quickly after Labor Day with the first frost. It's a favorite season for hiking due to the vibrant foliage and lack of bugs. The leaves change first in the High Peaks and northern Adirondacks. Peak color in these two regions usually occurs during the last week of September. Other parts of the park hold their color a week or two longer. Expect ice on the northern side of the taller mountains and be prepared for snow at any time after the first week in October.

Most of the hikes in this book make excellent winter hikes and snowshoeing routes, though not for the inexperienced. Adirondack winters are harsh, with snow and ice storms periodically halting wilderness travel. It's among the coldest places in the Lower 48, with temperatures dipping as low as minus-40 degrees Fahrenheit. If you plan a winter hike, be prepared with the right clothing, footwear, snowshoes, crampons and ski poles. Check the weather and avalanche conditions before venturing into the backcountry, particularly in the High Peaks region above tree line.

Mud season—April and May—is the only time of the year to avoid hiking in the Adirondacks. Snow can linger on the mountains and in sheltered valleys. Stay off the trails during mud season for the trails' sake. Many routes climb directly up slopes rather than around switchbacks, making them more susceptible to erosion from foot traffic when conditions are muddy.

Backcountry Checklist

Regardless of the time of year, whenever you head into the Adirondacks, you should expect to encounter high humidity and the chance of precipitation. Waterproof-breathable footwear, wool or wool-blend socks, and quick-drying, non-cotton apparel are *de riguere*. In addition, here's a list of essential items to put in your backpack. This is a fair-weather list. Winter hikers will need additional items:

- Bug repellent
- Rain gear
- Fleece or wool sweater
- Wool hat
- Ball cap
- Sunscreen
- Food
- Water (all trailside water sources carry risk of giardia)
- This book! (or a trail map)
- Compass
- First-aid kit
- Whistle
- Waterproof matches or a reliable lighter

- Flashlight or headlamp
- Swiss Army knife or other multi-tool
- Bandana
- Watch

Trail Contacts

In case of emergency, dial 911. *Note:* Mobile phone service in the Adirondacks outside of major towns is unreliable.

Adirondack Mountain Club (ADK): Member Services: 814 Goggins Rd., Lake George, NY 12845; (518) 668-4447. Lodging/Heart Lake Program Center: Adirondack Loj Rd., P.O. Box 867, Lake Placid, NY 12946; (518) 523-3441; www .adk.org

Adirondack Mountain Reserve-Ausable Club, 137 Ausable Rd., St. Huberts, NY 12943; (518) 576-4411; www.ausable club.org

Adirondack Trail Improvement Society (ATIS), P.O. Box 565, Keene Valley, NY 12943; www.atis-web.com

New York State Department of Environmental Conservation (NYSDEC): Division of Public Affairs and Education, 625 Broadway, Albany, NY 12233; (518) 402-8013. NYSDEC Region 5 Office (Adirondack Park), 1115 Rte. 86, P.O. Box 296, Ray Brook, NY 12977; (518) 897-1200; www.dec.ny .gov

Leave No Trace

The Adirondack Park is a big place, but if every visitor to its pristine backcountry left only a small mark, it would quickly be destroyed. As at home, do not litter—not even biodegradables such as orange peels. While they may degrade over time, it takes longer than you think, and they are not part of the park's natural ecosystem. At the same time, take only pictures. Picking a flower may seem harmless, but it could be an endangered species. Likewise, leave wildlife alone both for your safety and their survival.

While it is impossible to have zero impact as you pass through the Adirondack Park, here are some key ways to minimize evidence of your visit:

1. Leave with everything you brought in.
2. Leave no sign of your visit.
3. Leave the landscape as you found it.

One easy way to be a low-impact hiker is to simply stay on the trail. Walking around mud holes may keep your boots drier and cleaner, but it widens the trail over time. In addition, avoid taking shortcuts and cutting corners on switchbacks. It may save a few seconds here and there, but it increases erosion and leaves unsightly scars in the woods. Above tree line it is vital that you stay on the trail, walking on rock as much as possible. Fragile alpine plants grow very slowly, enduring the harsh mountaintop environment, but they cannot withstand trampling.

Finally, be considerate of others. Voices carry, particularly across bodies of water. Try to keep noise to a minimum so that all can enjoy the serenity of the wilderness.

For more information visit www. LNT.org.

Trail Finder

Best Hikes for Small Children
1. Baker Mountain
6. Mount Jo Loop
10. Mount Arab
14. Blue Mountain

Best Hikes for Dogs
1. Baker Mountain
2. Baxter Mountain
12. Saint Regis Mountain

Best Hikes to Views of the High Peaks
4. Cascade Mountain
5. Giant's Nubble via the Ridge Trail
7. Noonmark Mountain

Best Hikes to Bald Spots
4. Cascade Mountain
5. Giant's Nubble via the Ridge Trail
7. Noonmark Mountain

Best Wildflower Hikes
10. Mount Arab
11. Lyon Mountain
20. Black Bear Mountain

Best Hikes to Fire Towers

10. Mount Arab
11. Lyon Mountain
12. Saint Regis Mountain
13. Goodnow Mountain
14. Blue Mountain
17. Hadley Mountain
18. Kane Mountain
19. Bald Mountain (Rondaxe)
22. Poke-O-Moonshine

Best Hikes for Water Lovers

5. Giant's Nubble via the Ridge Trail
12. Saint Regis Mountain
15. Crane Mountain–Crane Pond Loop

Best Fall Foliage Hikes

12. Saint Regis Mountain
20. Black Bear Mountain
22. Poke-O-Moonshine

Map Legend

	Interstate Highway
	U.S. Highway
	State Highway
	Local Road
	Unpaved Road
	Railroad
	Featured Trail
	Trail
	Ladder/Stairs or Steps
	Body of Water
	River/Creek
	Marsh
	Boat launch
	Bridge
	Mountain/Peak
	Parking
	Picnic Area
	Point of Interest/Trailhead
	Restroom
	Tower
	Town
	Trailhead
	Viewpoint/Overlook
	Waterfall

High Peaks Region

While the High Peaks region of the Adirondacks is best known for its forty-six peaks over 4,000 feet in elevation, it also boasts numerous hikes with equally stunning views that don't surpass that lauded benchmark. In this section, you'll find Cascade Mountain, considered the easiest of the 4,000-footers as well as a number of other hikes more modest in terms of summit elevation, but superlative in enjoyment. With big rewards for minimal effort, these routes are perfect for a family outing, but don't expect solitude, as they attract many school groups and summer camps. Always be prepared with proper footwear, clothing, food, water, and emergency items when attempting any hikes in the High Peaks, no matter how easy they may sound. This area always has a high chance of extreme weather, twelve months of the year.

1 Baker Mountain

This small mountain offers a big reward and is a perfect kid-hike to a view of the mountains and lakes around Saranac Lake, with the Great Range in the distance to the southeast.

Total distance: 1.8 miles
Type of hike: Out and back
Highest point: 2,441 feet
Vertical gain: 843 feet

Approximate hiking time: 2 hours
Canine compatibility: Dog-friendly
Map: USGS Saranac Lake Quad

Finding the Trailhead: From NY 3 (Bloomingdale Avenue) in Saranac Lake, turn southeast on Pine Street. Go 0.1 mile, then turn left (east) on Forest Hill Avenue, which goes around Moody Pond. Go 0.6 mile to the trailhead on the northeast side of the pond. Park in the shallow turnouts by the trailhead. Trailhead GPS: N44 19.891' / W74 06.961'

The Hike

From the sign-in box at the trailhead, the broad, obvious path (red NYSDEC markers) enters the woods and soon begins to climb up a rock-strewn path. The trail is fairly steep at first, but the footing is good as you pass through a pretty hardwood forest filled with maples and poplars. The woods glow red and yellow in late September and early October.

At 0.3 mile the trail reaches a plateau, where the walking gets easier on a gentle incline. A few minutes later, it heads uphill again. Stone steps go up a ridge of rock in the woods and then rock slab. As birch and pine start to take over, pine needles carpet the trail around the rocks.

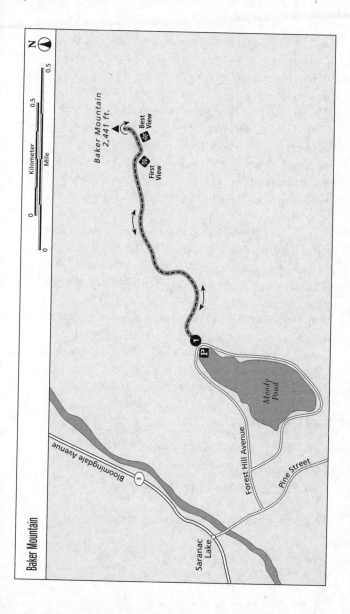

Baker Mountain

Baker Mountain
2,441 ft.

Best View

First View

Moody Pond

Forest Hill Avenue

Pine Street

Bloomingdale Avenue

Saranac Lake

3

P

1

Kilometer

Mile

0   0.5

0   0.5

N

After several long sections of slab, you begin to glimpse the neighboring hills and the village of Saranac Lake to your right (southwest). The many large rocks and boulders along the trail are fun for kids to climb. At 0.6 mile the footing becomes a mosaic of roots and the trail often braids. Stay to the right, hugging the edge of the hillside, closest to the view.

At 0.8 mile the trail stops climbing and breaks out of the forest canopy onto a rocky outcropping laden with wild blueberries. There is an excellent view to the right (west) of Lower Saranac Lake. The round lake to the south with the island in the middle is Lake Kiwassa. Lake Flower is the lake in the middle of the village.

From here the hike passes several rocky perches en route to the summit. The best view is about 300 feet farther up the trail. McKenzie Pond lies below McKenzie Mountain to the southeast, with the heart of the High Peaks crowning the horizon.

At 0.9 mile the trail reaches the top of the mountain. The benchmark is on the broad knob of rock under a few scrubby pine trees. The summit area is a web of unofficial trails. When in doubt, just head uphill and you'll get to the right place.

Return to the trailhead by the same route.

Miles and Directions

0.0 Start at the trailhead next to Moody Pond.

0.3 Traverse a small plateau and then continue climbing.

0.6 Stay to the right, hugging the side of the mountain nearest the view.

0.8 FIRST VIEW from a rocky outcropping! Continue to head uphill.

0.9 SUMMIT! Return to the trailhead by the same route.

1.8 Arrive back at the trailhead.

2 Baxter Mountain

A local favorite to a nice view of many landmark mountains in the High Peaks region.

Total distance: 2.6 miles
Type of hike: Out and back
Highest point: 2,341 feet
Vertical gain: 668 feet

Approximate hiking time: 2.5 hours
Canine compatibility: Dog-friendly
Map: USGS Keene Valley Quad

Finding the trailhead: From the junction of NY 73 and NY 9N, follow NY 9N east up a steep hill toward Elizabethtown. About 2.1 miles from the junction, look for the trailhead on your right, about 50 yards past Hurricane Road, on the opposite side of the road. Park on the wide shoulder of the road. Trailhead GPS: N44 13.253' / W73 44.971'

The Hike

There are three approaches up Baxter Mountain. This one (blue NYSDEC markers) is the shortest and easiest. The trail is smooth and flat as you enter the woods. It immediately passes through a power-line cut and then climbs easily through white birch, hemlock, and firs. It ascends some broad log steps as more hardwoods come into the mix, and then becomes steeper, though nothing harsh.

At 0.4 mile the trail flattens briefly, then bends sharply to the right (west) by a large hemlock partway up the next pitch. A little further, several switchbacks aid your ascent.

At 0.9 mile the path crosses a potentially muddy area on broad stones, then ascends more stones and roots. Soon it

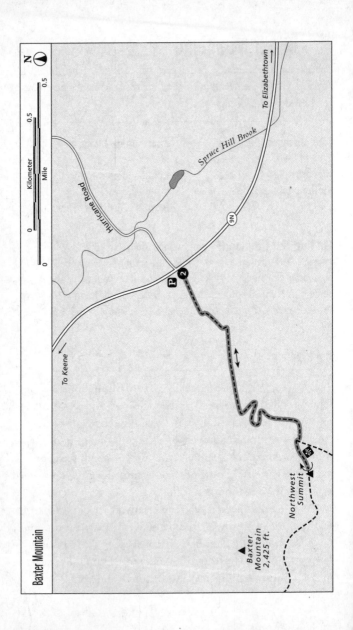

Baxter Mountain

Baxter Mountain
2,425 ft.

Northwest
Summit

Hurricane Road

Spruce Hill Brook

9N

To Keene

To Elizabethtown

P
2

N

0   0.5   Kilometer
0   0.5   Mile

comes to the junction with the Beede Road Trail. Bear right (north), still following the blue markers.

After a couple more switchbacks past a low rock outcropping, the trail climbs to the west up some slab. At 1.2 miles it breaks free of the canopy at a rocky perch laden with wild blueberries. You can see the fire tower atop Hurricane Mountain to your left. Nippletop is to the right, with Giant Mountain in between.

From the perch, bear right (north), uphill, not along the rock cliff, leaving the view to your back and crossing a state wild forest boundary. You are now in the Giant Mountain Wilderness. Climb up a short, steep, rocky section, then cross some slab to find the northwest summit of the mountain, your destination for this hike, at 1.3 miles. It's a small knob of smooth rock surrounded by trees, but there is a nice ledge just below it with a beautiful view. Giant Mountain dominates the panorama to the south. Nippletop and a number of the other High Peaks lie to the southwest. Hurricane Mountain is to the east, easily identified by its fire tower.

Return to the trailhead by the same route.

Miles and Directions

0.0 Start at the trailhead on the side of NY 9N.

0.4 Pass a large hemlock and begin to ascend through a number of switchbacks.

0.9 Cross a muddy section on broad stones. Then bear right at the junction with Beede Road Trail.

1.2 Enjoy the view and the blueberries from a rocky perch.

1.3 NORTHWEST SUMMIT! Return by the same route.

2.6 Arrive back at the trailhead.

3 The Brothers

An Adirondack classic to a series of three rock ledges on the shoulder of Big Slide Mountain that rewards with multiple views and acres of wild blueberries.

Total distance: 5.2 miles
Type of Hike: Out and back
Highest point: 3,681 feet
Vertical gain: 2,157 feet

Approximate hiking time: 5 hours
Canine compatibility: Dog-friendly
Map: USGS Keene Valley Quad

Finding the Trailhead: From NY 73 in Keene Valley, turn right (west) on Adirondack Street. Go 1.6 miles. The road narrows and turns to dirt, becoming Johns Brook Lane, which ends at the trailhead called The Garden. If the parking lot is full, there is an overflow lot at Marcy airfield, north of Keene Valley on NY 73, with a hiker shuttle to The Garden. (Fee for parking.) Trailhead GPS: N44 11.224' / W73 48.875'

The Hike

The hike to The Brothers, a series of three ledges laden with blueberries and impressive views, is part of the more epic 10-miler to the summit of Big Slide (4,199 feet). Some maps show The Brothers as a separate peak, but it is really a shoulder of massive Big Slide. *Note:* If you decide to continue to Big Slide, the climb above The Brothers to the summit of Big Slide is not dog-friendly due to ladders and steep rock chimneys.

Each Brother is a lovely destination in itself, so you can decide how far you want to go based on how you feel at that moment and the weather. First Brother and Second Brother reward with superb views. Third Brother, the highest point described here, has a wooded summit except for a good view of the summit of Big Slide.

From the trailhead, take the right trail (blue NYSDEC markers) toward Porter Mountain and The Brothers. It's a steady climb from the start. The footing is good at first, with only some roots crisscrossing the trail through a forest dominated by maple and paper birch.

At 0.3 mile the trail to Porter Mountain departs to the right. Continue straight toward the first of the three Brothers. The trail ascends moderately to a height of land, then dips down over a streamlet, which might be dry. From here, the climb continues, soon becoming more persistent and rocky.

At 0.7 mile the trail opens on a rock shoulder of The Brothers where there is a view to the southwest of neighboring Rooster Comb Mountain across a narrow valley. From here, the trail hangs on the side of the mountain for a short way, then bends back into the woods around a rock outcropping.

At 1.5 miles, you reach the First Brother. The view into the High Peaks is eye-popping and just gets better as you go higher. Wild blueberries are everywhere in early August. It's tempting to pick a ledge, eat blueberries, and forget about going further.

The trail bends back into the woods, descending briefly, then returns to the edge of the cliff, climbing again. At 1.8 miles, you reach the Second Brother, where the view is almost 360 degrees. You can see the hump of Big Slide ahead

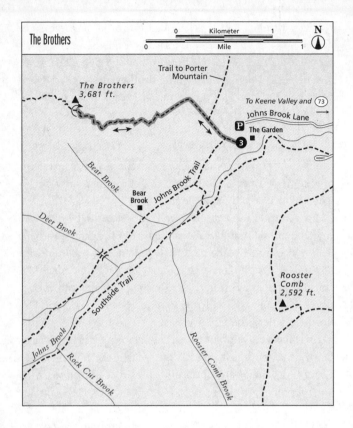

to the west. *Note:* Although the painted blazes on the rocks are yellow, the NYSDEC markers remain blue.

The trail continues through a small depression and then climbs persistently, reaching the Third Brother at 2.6 miles.

Return by the same route.

Miles and Directions

0.0 Start at The Garden. Take the trail toward Porter Mountain and The Brothers (blue NYSDEC markers).

0.3 At the junction with the trail to Porter Mountain, continue straight toward The Brothers.

0.7 Pass over a rock shoulder with a view of Rooster Comb Mountain.

1.5 FIRST BROTHER! Continue toward the Second Brother.

1.8 SECOND BROTHER! Continue toward Third Brother.

2.6 THIRD BROTHER! Return by the same route.

5.2 Arrive back at The Garden.

4 Cascade Mountain

The easiest of the Adirondack 4,000-footers and a great "starter" hike whether your ultimate goal is to become a "46-er" or just stand atop one of them and look at most of the others. It also has wonderful views of Lake Champlain and the Green Mountains of Vermont.

Total distance: 4.8 miles
Type of Hike: Out and back
Highest point: 4,098 feet
Vertical gain: 1,899 feet

Approximate hiking time: 4.5 hours
Canine compatibility: Dog-friendly. Dogs must be on leash.
Map: USGS Keene Valley Quad

Finding the Trailhead: From the junction of NY 73 and Old Military Road by the fairgrounds in Lake Placid, follow NY 73 east for 6 miles (past the Olympic ski jumping complex). The trailhead is on the right (south) side of the road at the second of three small parking areas, just before Upper Cascade Lake. Trailhead GPS: N44 13.136' / W73 53.254'

The Hike

Cascade Mountain is a popular hike, so it's best to get an early start if you want a parking spot in one of the three turnouts by the trailhead. This is a good one for older kids and for less-experienced hikers looking for a big reward without serious mileage. It's also the perfect hike for the road-weary looking for some exercise after a long drive into the Adirondack Park but without a big time commitment—plus you get credit for bagging a 4,000-footer.

Note: Though Cascade Mountain is considered entry-level by seasoned hikers, it is still a 4,000-footer, with an exposed summit. Expect wind, and be prepared for cold temperatures and sudden weather changes even on a fair summer day. In addition, there is a lot of open rock, which can be slick when wet. Save this one for a nice day.

From the trailhead, descend a log-framed staircase and then cross four short footbridges to reach the sign-in box. This well-used trail follows red NYSDEC markers, ascending immediately from the box. There are lots of rocks and roots on the eroded trail, but they seem more like steps than inconvenient obstacles. Numerous water bars and well-placed stones help keep this popular trail in shape.

The trail climbs at a comfortable rate, heading south through a mixed northern forest of birch, striped maple, and beech. There are breaks in the ascent, first to cross a stream that flows down a pretty, mossy cascade just above the trail, and second to pass through a mud hole on large stepping stones. From the mud hole, the path heads deeper into the forest to the southeast. Soon it begins to climb steadily again and become rockier.

At 0.7 mile the pitch gets steeper, although two dozen stone steps aid the climb. It levels off as you pass a pointed-top boulder next to the trail, and then turns upward once again, becoming rocky and eroded again. As you near the boreal zone, birch "pillars" beckon you upward, with firs and other evergreens filling in the gaps, and the climb becomes more sustained.

At 1 mile the trail swings northeast and some slab appears underfoot. You can see more sky through the thinning canopy. The pitch moderates a little and then levels off briefly as you cross a wide mud pit, then it resumes its aggressive ascent.

At 1.3 miles, after one particularly washed-out slabby area, the trail bends to the east, passing a flat-top rock. There's no view, but it's a good place to take a break. Above the rock the trail eases as it winds through forest. You begin to sense the higher elevation, with some sky to either side of you. You are on a high buttress of the mountain. A cool breeze blows through the firs and the sporadic weather-beaten birches.

The eroded trail climbs steadily, eventually heading up a length of steep slab and then breaking onto an open rock at 1.8 miles. Marcy looms large to the west, and there is a great view of the ski jumps and Lake Placid to the north.

The trail reenters spindly trees, continuing to the northeast over more slab and mud. At 2.1 miles the trail forks at a broad, flat rock. The right fork goes to Porter Mountain. Bear left, following the red markers and the arrow toward Cascade Mountain.

The trail becomes fairly level, soon passing through a small grassy clearing. The trees end just ahead. Follow the yellow printed blazes and rock cairns up the expansive bald rock toward the summit. It's steep, requiring some scrambling and some easy friction climbing in places.

The trail ends at the summit at 2.4 miles, a broad, long ridge with many places to enjoy the view and have a picnic even if there are lots of people there. You can see the fire tower on Hurricane Mountain to the east, Memorial Highway snaking up Whiteface Mountain to the north, Lake Placid village and lake to the northwest, and a mesmerizing number of 4,000-footers to the south including the famous Great Range (Gothics, Armstrong, Upper Wolfjaw, and Lower Wolfjaw).

Return to the trailhead by the same route.

Cascade Mountain

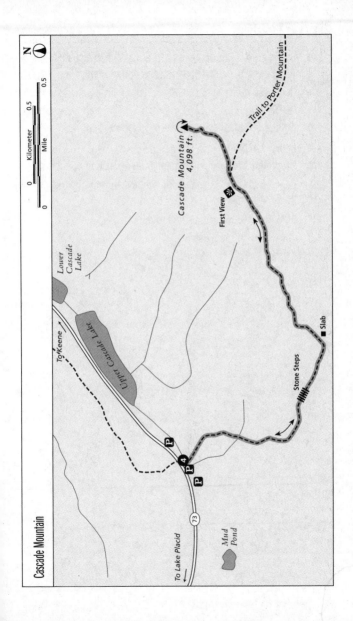

N

0   Kilometer   0.5
0   Mile   0.5

To Keene

Lower Cascade Lake

Upper Cascade Lake

Cascade Mountain
4,098 ft.

Trail to Porter Mountain

First View

Slab

Stone Steps

73

To Lake Placid

Mud Pond

P 4
P
P

Miles and Directions

0.0 Start at the trailhead. Descend the log-framed stairs into the woods and cross four short lengths of puncheon.

0.7 Climb two dozen stone steps and then pass a pointed boulder.

1.0 Swing northeast as slab appears underfoot.

1.3 Pass a flat-top rock.

1.8 Reach the first view on the hike, from a patch of open rock.

2.1 Bear left toward the summit at the junction with the trail to Porter Mountain.

2.4 SUMMIT! Return by the same route.

4.8 Arrive back at the trailhead.

5 Giant's Nubble via the Ridge Trail

A pleasant hike to a remote tarn and a rocky lookout on Giant Mountain, great for those who want a view but don't want to scale an entire 4,000-footer.

Total distance: 3.0 miles
Type of hike: Out and back
Highest point: 2,743 feet
Vertical gain: 1,063 feet

Approximate hiking time: 3 hours
Canine compatibility:
Dog-friendly
Map: USGS Keene Valley Quad

Finding the trailhead: From the junction of NY 73 and Ausable Road (the road to the Ausable Club) in Saint Huberts, head south on NY 73 for 2 miles. Go past the second entrance to Ausable Road and the parking area for the Roaring Brook Trail. The trailhead for the Ridge Trail is just past Chapel Pond on the left (north) side of the road.

If approaching from I-87, take exit 30 onto NY 73 and US 9 north, go for 2.1 miles. Where NY 73 and US 9 split, continue on NY 73 for another 3.0 miles. Trailhead GPS: N44 08.318' / W73 44.597'

The Hike

Giant's Nubble is a knob of rock on the southern side of Giant Mountain, the tallest peak in the Giant Mountain Wilderness. There are two approaches to the Nubble, one from the Roaring Brook Trail, the other from the Ridge Trail, which are 1.3 miles apart on NY 73. If you have two cars, you can start at one end and hike to the other, which is about the same mileage as doing it as an out-and-back. With a car drop, you can also take in the tall, beautiful waterfall on Roaring Brook. *Note:* It is not a good idea to walk beside NY 73, which winds through a narrow ravine between the two trailheads, with a guardrail on one side and a steep hillside on the other.

The route described here is via the Ridge Trail, as it not only goes to the Nubble but also to Giant Washbowl, a serene mountain tarn that is the largest body of water in the Giant Mountain Wilderness.

From the trailhead, the path follows blue NYSDEC markers east into the woods over a couple of small footbridges to the sign-in box. From there it climbs moderately through a hardwood forest typical of the Adirondacks at lower elevations. In early July, wild raspberries bloom profusely along the trail.

The path bends left over an unreliable streamlet and then angles to the northeast following the streambed. Though the trail is strewn with rocks and roots, the footing is generally good as you climb. During the summer, patches of white wood sorrel flowers burst from green clover-like leaves, brightening the ground here and there.

Soon the trail gets rockier and steeper. It crosses the streamlet again, angling up the slope. Everything around you seems green and lush. After several switchbacks and some stone steps up a particularly steep pitch, it comes alongside the streamlet again, then crosses it. The slope eases a bit, crossing some sections of slab, heading north across a height of land. This is the top of the rock wall on the left side of the ravine above NY 73. Once atop this plateau the road noise seems far below and quickly fades away.

At 0.5 mile there is a nice rock perch with a view of Chapel Pond below and the Great Range (Gothics, Armstrong, Upper Wolfjaw, and Lower Wolfjaw Mountains) to the west. From here the trail dips as it continues north back into the woods, away from Chapel Pond.

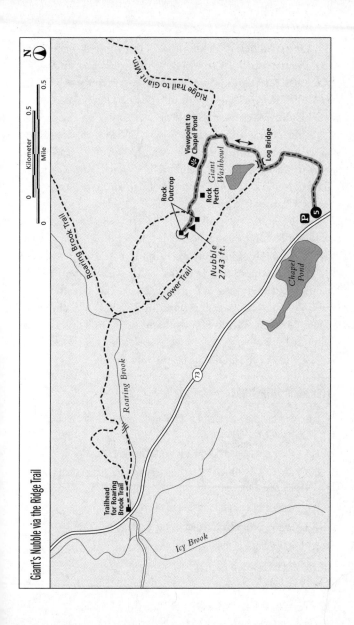

Giant's Nubble via the Ridge Trail

N

Kilometer
0   0.5
Mile
0   0.5

Roaring Brook Trail

Ridge Trail to Giant Mtn.

Viewpoint to Chapel Pond

Rock Outcrop

Giant Washbowl

Rock Perch

Log Bridge

Nubble
2743 ft.

Lower Trail

P 5

Roaring Brook

73

Chapel Pond

Trailhead for Roaring Brook Trail

Icy Brook

Almost immediately, at 0.6 mile, it comes to Giant Wash-bowl. Nestled below a cliff, the Washbowl is a 4.2-acre pond that the state stocks with brook trout. Frogs chirp among the waterlilies that speckle the pond. It's a pleasant place to take a break if the rock perch you just passed is populated. There is a primitive campsite just beyond the pond on the right.

After taking a break to enjoy the Washbowl, continue a short way to the junction with the less-traveled trail to the Nubble at 0.8 mile. The trail climbs in spurts until it reaches Giant's Nubble, crossing sections of slab and several openings in the weathered trees.

At 1.5 miles the trail climbs an obvious rock highpoint, the Nubble! From the Nubble, Chapel Pond lies directly below you. Round Mountain is immediately across NY 73, forming the opposite side of the valley, with Noonmark just behind, but the eye is drawn to the Great Range, the string of 4,000-footers just to the right (northwest). The summit of Giant Mountain with its trademark slides are behind you to the northeast.

Return to the trailhead by the same route.

Miles and Directions

- **0.0** Start at the trailhead for the Ridge Trail up Giant Mountain (blue NYSDEC markers).
- **0.5** Pass a rock perch with a view of Chapel Pond.
- **0.6** GIANT WASHBOWL! Continue a short way farther on the Ridge Trail.
- **0.8** Turn left (west) on the trail to the Nubble.
- **1.5** GIANT'S NUBBLE! Return by the same route.
- **3.0** Arrive back at the trailhead.

6 Mount Jo Loop

A short, kid-friendly hike along an interpretive trail to a big view of the High Peaks.

Total distance: 1.9 miles
Type of hike: Lollipop
Highest point: 2,876 feet
Vertical gain: 651 feet

Approximate hiking time: 2 hours
Canine compatibility: Dog-friendly. Dogs should be on leash.
Map: USGS North Elba Quad

Finding the Trailhead: From Lake Placid, take NY 73 east toward Keene. Go 1.5 miles past the entrance to the Olympic ski jump complex, then turn right (south) on Adirondack Loj Road. Go 4.6 miles to the end of the road and the sizable hiker parking area at Adirondak Loj. The trailhead is on the side of the parking lot directly in front of the information building. *Note:* Fee for parking, which is discounted for members of the Adirondack Mountain Club. Trailhead GPS: N44 11.094' / W73 57.810'

The Hike

Mount Jo is a small hike that delivers a close-in look at many of the tallest mountains in the Adirondacks. Its trailhead shares a parking lot with the trailheads to Mount Marcy, Algonquin Peak, Wright Peak, and a number of the other giants.

Originally called Bear Mountain, it was renamed in the 1870s for Josephine Schofield, fiancée of Henry Van Hoevenberg, the Adirondack guide who masterminded the original Adirondak Loj and who laid out many of the trails that begin here. Schofield and Van Hoevenberg were engaged after camping with a group of friends by Upper Ausable Lake during the summer of 1877. Schofield's parents were adamantly opposed to the engagement. She died mysteriously before the marriage, and the heartbroken Van Hoevenberg named Mount Jo in her memory while building the home beside Heart Lake that they had planned to build together. However, instead of a modest home, he built an enormous log lodge, the original Adirondak Loj, considered the largest free-standing log structure in the country at the time.

In 1903 a forest fire burned the lodge and most of the surrounding forest. As with other bald peaks in the Adirondack Park that are technically below tree line, the summit of Mount Jo remains open because the soil quickly eroded away after the fire cleared the flora at this low but exposed point. Today the trail takes you through mature second-growth forest then ends at a fine viewpoint.

Mount Jo is popular among school groups and summer camps, so expect company at the summit. It follows an interpretive trail. You can buy an inexpensive brochure for the interpretive trail at the nature museum, a small cabin near the edge of Heart Lake, a short way into the hike. There are two approaches to the summit, the Long Trail and the Short Trail, which combined make a nice loop as described here.

The trailhead to Mount Jo also gives access to Rocky Falls, Indian Pass, and the Heart Lake Loop. It begins as a flat manicured path (red NYSDEC markers), passing several buildings tucked into the trees on the Adirondak Loj campus. At 0.2 mile, it comes to a T near the edge of Heart Lake. The left path returns to Adirondak Loj. Turn right (northwest), passing the nature museum. In another 100 feet, the trail to Rocky Falls and Indian Pass departs to the left. Turn right again, up a couple of rough stone steps and onto a "normal" footpath.

From the sign-in box, the well-used trail ascends steadily over rocks and roots, now following orange ADK markers. This is the nature trail, with numbered signposts along the way. At 0.4 mile, the trail splits. The Long Trail, to the left, is 0.7 mile to the summit. The Short Trail, to the right, is 0.4 mile to the summit. You will close the loop here later. Turn right, following the Short Trail.

The Short Trail turns uphill, heading north and following a streamlet. It soon flattens across a muddy area. Many stepping stones help keep your feet dry. After crossing the streamlet, the path turns upward again onto drier ground, though the footing is somewhat rougher. The trail weaves between boulders, called "glacial erratics" that were deposited during the last ice age, and soon climbs beside a low cliff wall speckled with moss and lichen. The rock is discolored brown by minerals left behind by the constant drip of water.

At 0.6 mile, an arrow painted on a wall of rock points the way to the left. The trail bends around the wall and continues its ascent, now rather vertically but aided by sections of stone steps. The climb eases briefly then continues upward on more steps, angling to the northwest along the hillside. After yet another stone staircase, the trail pops onto open rock. You can see Algonquin Peak behind you before the trail bends left, entering a corridor of spruce and fir.

The trail soon passes a short spur on the right to a better lookout. Heart Lake lies below you. Mount Marcy is now visible to the southwest, with the Great Range to the left and Avalanche Pass to the right of Marcy. From here, it's still uphill, but easier as you come to the upper junction with the Long Trail at 0.7 mile. Bear right, continuing uphill.

The path flattens as it reaches the summit plateau, then swings right (east) at the bottom of a rocky hump. This is not the summit. The trail crosses a muddy area, then dips over a two-log footbridge. After a couple of short, rocky scrambles, you arrive at the true summit at 0.8 mile.

The top of Mount Jo is a rock knob with a spectacular view. Algonquin looms above Heart Lake, with a string of the other High Peaks, including Cascade, Porter, Big Slide, Phelps, Basin, Marcy, Colden, Street, and Nye, among the impressive line of mountains before you. The view is not quite 360 degrees. To see the mountains to the north, mainly Whiteface, you need to walk among the trees in that direction.

To return to the trailhead, retrace back to the upper junction of the Long Trail and the Short Trail at 0.9 mile. Go straight (west), heading down the steeper route, though it is only steeper than the Short Trail for a short way and much less rocky. The Long Trail is mostly joint-friendly dirt, with some roots across the path. It becomes more rock-strewn and eventually rather eroded like a streambed but only for a short section.

At the bottom of the slope, the trail bends left (south) onto smooth, dry ground, passing under a 20-foot rock wall before coming to the junction with the Rock Garden Trail at 1.1 miles. Go straight (south) at the junction.

The trail passes through a muddy area, then continues downhill over some slab. It rolls gently up and down on a traverse to the east until you close the loop at the lower junction with the Short Trail at 1.5 miles. From here, retrace the path past Heart Lake and the nature museum, returning to the trailhead at 1.9 miles.

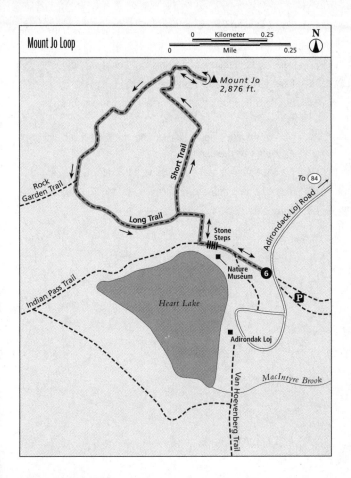

Mount Jo Loop

| 0 | Kilometer | 0.25 |
| 0 | Mile | 0.25 |

N

▲ Mount Jo
2,876 ft.

Rock Garden Trail

Short Trail

Long Trail

To (84)

Adirondack Loj Road

Stone Steps

Indian Pass Trail

Nature Museum

6

P

Heart Lake

Adirondak Loj

Van Hoevenberg Trail

MacIntyre Brook

Miles and Directions

0.0 Start at the trailhead by the toll booth at the entrance to the Adirondak Loj parking lots.

0.2 Turn right, passing the nature museum, then in another 100 feet turn right again up stone steps.

0.4 Turn right on the Short Trail at the lower junction with the Long Trail.

0.6 Bear left at the arrow around the low stone wall.

0.7 Bear right at the upper junction with the Long Trail.

0.8 SUMMIT! Retrace back to the upper junction with the Long Trail.

0.9 Go straight at the upper junction with the Long Trail, following the Long Trail downhill.

1.1 Continue straight at the junction with the Rock Garden Trail.

1.5 Close the loop at the lower junction with the Short Trail.

1.9 Arrive back at the trailhead.

7 Noonmark Mountain

A steady climb to a round, bald summit with many views of the 4,000-footers not only from the summit, but also from the open rock along much of the upper route.

Total distance: 5.8 miles
Type of hike: Out and back
Highest point: 3,471 feet
Vertical gain: 2,177 feet
Approximate hiking time: 6 hours

Canine compatibility: Not dog-friendly due to ladders and several rock chimneys. Dogs are not allowed on Ausable Club and Adirondack Mountain Reserve lands.
Map: USGS Keene Valley Quad

Finding the Trailhead: From the bridge over Johns Brook in Keene Valley, travel 3.3 miles east on NY 73 to Saint Huberts. At the second junction with Ausable Road, turn right. Go about 100 yards. The trailhead parking lot is on the left. This is the same parking lot for the hikes to Mount Colvin and the Great Range. Parking is not permitted along Ausable Road. Trailhead parking GPS: N44 08.982' / W73 46.078'

The Hike

Noonmark Mountain is so named because it is due south of Keene Valley and marks the noon position of the sun. It's a sturdy 2,177 feet of vertical gain in only 2.9 miles, but there is a lot to see along the way as you scramble up rocks and ladders.

From the hiker parking lot, continue up Ausable Road on foot. This dirt road is private, one of two ways into the heart of the Ausable Club, but a public right-of-way for hikers. At

0.1 mile, a trail to Round Mountain departs to the left. Continue to follow Ausable Road farther onto the club's grounds.

At 0.6 mile, at the corner of the golf course, the trailhead for the Noonmark Trail, also known as the Stimson Trail, is on your left. It is named for Henry Stimson, who created the route. Turn left onto the Stimson Trail, which is still a dirt road. After passing a couple of driveways, the road turns sharply uphill to the right. Continue straight, following the yellow markers and the trail sign with an arrow pointing to the left.

Pass another house and then bear right at the next arrow and the trail marker onto a footpath at 0.8 mile. The trail traverses the side of a hill, soon meeting an older path. The route is wide and obvious with good footing. It provides a pleasant stroll through mature hemlocks with birch trees and other hardwoods in the airy forest mix.

After crossing the boundary onto state land, the climb becomes more obvious but is still moderate. A sizable stream (unreliable) lies below you on the left in a small gorge. At 1.1 miles, you come to the junction with the Dix Trail, which is both to Dix Mountain and a second route to Round Mountain. Bear right, staying on the Stimson Trail, following the red markers.

The climb now becomes steep and direct, but it is well maintained. At 1.5 miles, the trail bends sharply right (north), up a stone staircase, allowing a brief respite from the persistent ascent. You feel closer to the sky, though you are still under the canopy. A couple of welcome switchbacks lie above the steps, and then the steady upward climb resumes.

At 1.7 miles, there's a beautiful view of Giant Mountain across the gap and many wild blueberries at your feet. Above this first perch, the trail enters the boreal forest and becomes a patchwork of slab and ledge. The trees thin as you leave the view of Giant Mountain behind. There are more large rocks to scramble up as you ascend a high shoulder of the mountain. From here, the trail continues through the conifers and tons of blueberries.

At 2.2 miles, you come to the first of two ladders, a short one up a half-buried boulder. The ladders are separated by a rock chimney and a view of the Great Range, plus a look at the summit of Noonmark as you climb. The second ladder aids the ascent up a longer rock chimney. Finish the climb up this particularly vertical spot using the steps and crack in the rock.

The route is now more open in a subalpine zone with many lookouts as you scramble up more rock. At 2.9 miles, the trail suddenly meets a 15-foot-high vertical wall. Head right to get on top of it, which is the summit of Noonmark. There is a 360-degree view, but you can't see it all at once due to a few low spruce trees. Nippletop, with its slides, lies to the southwest. Giant Mountain stands tall beyond Round Mountain to the northeast. Mount Marcy and the Great Range lie to the west of the narrow valley that runs southwest from the Ausable Club.

Return by the same route.

Miles and Directions

0.0   Start at the hiker parking lot on Ausable Road, then walk up Ausable Road (dirt).

0.1   Pass the trailhead for Round Mountain.

0.6   At the corner of the golf course, turn left at the trailhead sign for Noonmark Mountain, also a dirt road.

0.8   Follow the arrow straight onto a footpath when the dirt road bends sharply right.

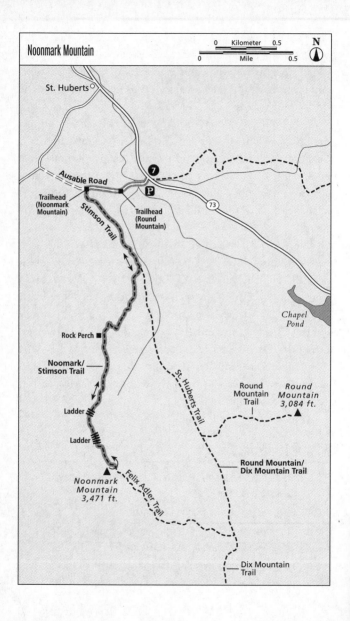

Noonmark Mountain

0 — Kilometer — 0.5
0 — Mile — 0.5

N

St. Huberts

Ausable Road

7

73

Trailhead
(Noonmark
Mountain)

P

Trailhead
(Round
Mountain)

Stimson Trail

Chapel
Pond

Rock Perch ■

**Noomark/
Stimson Trail**

St. Huberts Trail

Round
Mountain
Trail

*Round
Mountain
3,084 ft.* ▲

Ladder

Ladder

**Round Mountain/
Dix Mountain Trail**

*Noonmark
Mountain
3,471 ft.* ▲

Felix Adler Trail

Dix Mountain
Trail

1.1 Turn right on the Stimson Trail.

1.5 Bend sharply right (north) up a stone staircase.

1.7 Head around the base of a rock outcropping, then up its right side to a view of Giant Mountain.

2.2 Climb the first of two ladders.

2.9 SUMMIT of Noonmark! Return by the same route.

5.8 Arrive back at the hiker parking lot.

8 Balanced Rock (Pitchoff Mountain)

An invigorating hike to a balancing boulder on a broad rock plateau with a view of Mount Marcy and other Adirondack 4,000-footers.

Total distance: 2.6 miles
Type of hike: Out and back
Highest point: 2,950 feet
Vertical gain: 775 feet

Approximate hiking time: 2.5 hours
Canine compatibility: Dog-friendly
Map: USGS Keene Valley Quad

Finding the trailhead: From the junction of NY 73 and Old Military Road (by the fairgrounds in Lake Placid), go 8.8 miles on NY 73 east. Leave a car in the small parking lot across the road from the Pitchoff East trailhead, which is on the left (north) side of the road. Trailhead GPS: N44 14.624' / W73 50.751'

Drive 2.7 miles back toward Lake Placid. Park in one of the three small lots by the Cascade Mountain trailhead just above Cascade Lake. Begin the hike at the trailhead for the Sentinel Range Wilderness, on the opposite (north) side of the road. Trailhead GPS: N44 13.157' / W73 53.218'

The Hike

The Balanced Rock is on a shoulder of Pitchoff Mountain, which lies at the edge of the Sentinel Range Wilderness. It's a lovely hike to a curious boulder that seems to defy gravity. It's a perfect first hike with kids due to this geologic curiosity. It's also a good choice if you are pressed for time, but want to get a little exercise and see a nice view.

Following the red NYSDEC markers, the hike leaves the side of NY 73 up a short, steep staircase. From the sign-in box, it's a moderate ascent up the hillside on an obvious footpath.

After a short, steep pitch, the trail levels off, then runs northeast, parallel to NY 73. You can glimpse Cascade Mountain and Upper Cascade Lake through the trees to your right.

At 0.5 mile, a short spur on the right takes you to the first lookout, mainly an unobstructed view of Cascade Mountain and Lakes, with Algonquin Peak poking up to the right.

At 0.7 mile, there is a better view from another lookout, with Mounts Colden and Wright and the tip of Mount Marcy added to the mix. From here the trail turns uphill, scrambling over rocks in spots. It levels off again as it nears the edge of the long cliff line. Yellow coltsfoot and oxeye daisies bloom along the trail in late June.

After another downhill dip, the trail turns away from Cascade Mountain and begins climbing among small boulders, then up an old short slide. As you enter the shrubs near the top of the slide, the trail comes to a T with an old route that is now blocked. Look back for a great view of Algonquin Peak. The trail dips again, then climbs steadily northeast and becomes more eroded, though nothing drastic.

At 1.2 miles a sign that says merely VIEW marks the short path to Balanced Rock. Turn right, crossing open bedrock toward Cascade Mountain. Blueberries, wild cranberries (lingonberries), wildflowers, and lichens color the cracks in the slab as you approach Balanced Rock at 1.3 miles.

Beyond the rock, the view is a spectacular panorama, with the fire tower on Hurricane in the distance to the far left (southeast); the Olympic bobsled run to the far right;

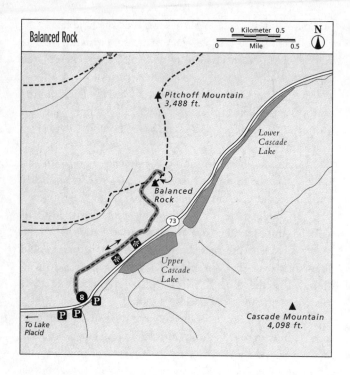

0 Kilometer 0.5

0   Mile   0.5

N

Pitchoff Mountain
3,488 ft.

Lower
Cascade
Lake

Balanced
Rock

73

Upper
Cascade
Lake

8

P P P

← To Lake
Placid

Cascade Mountain
4,098 ft.

and Cascade, Big Slide, Marcy, Colden, and Algonquin filling most of the view in between. The summit of Pitchoff is also visible above you to the north.

Return by the same route.

Miles and Directions

0.0 Climb the stairs at the trailhead next to NY 73, across from the Cascade Mountain trailhead.

0.5 Take the short spur to the first lookout, mainly of Cascade Mountain and Cascade Lakes.

0.7 Pass a second viewpoint, this time of Mounts Colden, Wright, and Marcy.

1.2 Turn right following the VIEW sign.

1.3 BALANCED ROCK! Retrace back to the trailhead.

2.6 Arrive back at the trailhead.

9 Rooster Comb

An enjoyable hike through pleasant woods to a close-in view of the Adirondacks giants.

Total distance: 5.2 miles
Type of hike: Out and back
Highest point: 2,592 feet
Vertical gain: 1,556 feet

Approximate hiking time: 4.5 hours
Canine compatibility: Dog-friendly
Map: USGS Keene Valley Quad

Finding the Trailhead: From the bridge over Johns Brook in Keene Valley, go 0.6 mile on NY 73 east (actually south at this point). The trailhead and substantial parking lot is on the right (west) side of the road at the south end of the village. Trailhead GPS: N44 11.124'/ W73 47.226'

The Hike

Rooster Comb is a lesser peak compared to its 4,000-foot neighbors, but it offers spectacular close-up views of those neighbors as well as the valley below for a rock perch near the summit.

From the parking area, follow the yellow NYSDEC markers over a long, well-constructed footbridge across a boggy backwater. The smooth, obvious trail, runs alongside the marsh and then a lovely pond which is adjacent to a school. This first section of the hike is part of the school's nature trail and a public right-of-way, however the woods on your left are private land.

At the junction at the southwest corner of the pond by a half-buried stone foundation, continue straight, heading deeper into the forest and crossing into the High Peaks Wilderness. The trail then begins to climb, aided by stone steps. The ascent is steady under towering hemlocks with little undergrowth. The trees seem like random pillars holding up the sky and provide cool shade on a warm day.

Hardwoods and more undergrowth soon reenter the forest mix as the trail winds up a half-dozen switchbacks. At 0.7 mile, you come to the junction with the trail from Snow Mountain. Bear right (straight), continuing to the southwest and following the yellow markers.

The steady climb levels off on a narrow woods road. The footing is nice—smooth dirt—and noticeably wider than a footpath. The route terraces the hillside, then turns 90 degrees left where logs and sticks block the way. After the turn, it becomes a regular footpath again, heading upward on the usual mix of scattered rocks and roots, though nothing too extreme.

A few minutes later the trail crosses a stream, which could be a small trickle after a dry spell, and bends to the right (west). Then it swings left (south) and eases, traversing through dense maples and beeches, as it continues upward on a moderate grade.

At 2 miles, the Hedgehog Mountain Trail departs to the left. This is another trail to Snow Mountain. Bear right (straight) uphill, now following blue NYSDEC markers. The path goes around an enormous glacial erratic, then dips and traverses to the northeast. It passes under a 25-foot-high rock wall, then climbs some rock steps by another rock outcropping. After a couple of switchbacks, you start to feel the elevation gain as you glimpse a nearby ridge through the trees.

At 2.2 miles, the trail reaches a T. Bear right (northeast) toward Valley View Ledge on a smooth descent, reaching the ledge at 2.3 miles. The view of Keene Valley and Marcy Field is quite pleasing. You can also see the fire tower atop Hurricane Mountain to the east across the valley. The ledges of The Brothers and the hulk of Big Slide dominate the view to the north.

Retrace your steps back to the main trail, bearing right (west), uphill, to continue to Rooster Comb's summit. The final approach to the summit is through classic boreal forest as evidenced by the low spindly conifers and birches. The trail traverses to the south, then bends sharply right, up a short but steep bit of slab. It continues to climb more persistently below some ledges, then turns sharply right again up a tall, steep staircase-like ladder.

After a fun scramble up another ledgy area, you get a great view to the east into Giant Mountain's huge cirque just beyond Round Mountain. NY 73 winds past Chapel Pond along the valley floor like a gray ribbon below you.

After a short eroded section and several long lengths of slab, you come to the summit area at 2.7 miles. Head southwest to the open ledge and an awesome view of Giant to the east, Noonmark to the south, and Marcy to the southwest. It's not a 360-degree view, but the close proximity of these big peaks more than makes up for the partial panorama.

Retrace back to the junction with the spur to Valley Ledge at 3 miles, then continue downhill retracing the route and arriving back at the trailhead at 5.2 miles.

Miles and Directions

- **0.0** Start at the trailhead beside NY 73 on the southern side of Keene.
- **0.7** Bear right at the junction with the trail from Snow Mountain, heading uphill toward Rooster Comb.
- **1.1** Turn 90 degrees left, leaving the woods road.

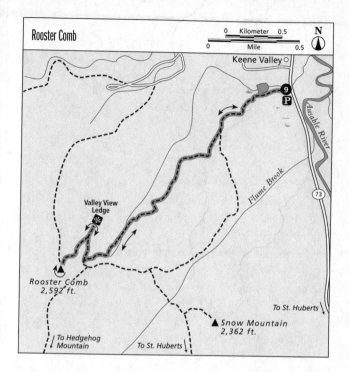

2.0 Bear right at the upper junction with the trail to Snow Mountain (left) and Hedgehog Mountain (straight), heading toward Rooster Comb.

2.2 Turn right toward Valley View Ledge.

2.3 VALLEY VIEW LEDGE! Retrace to the trail junction and continue straight (southwest) toward the summit.

2.7 SUMMIT of Rooster Comb! Return by the same route, skipping the spur to Valley View Ledge.

5.2 Arrive back at the trailhead and parking area.

Northern Region

The farther you go in the Northern Adirondacks—away from the center of the Adirondack Park—the flatter the land becomes. While the region doesn't have the dramatic topography, nor the multitude of bare summits found in other parts of the Adirondack Park, there are still several interesting peaks to climb.

Be aware that this is a popular area for hunting bear and deer in the fall. Hunting is permitted on all public land within the Adirondack Park, so it's a good idea to wear brightly colored clothing if you are hiking here from mid-September through December 31.

The biggest hazard to hikers is death by mosquito. Not really, but the insect population thrives on the abundance of water in the region. Some people wear bug netting, but a ball cap and a coating of bug repellent with at least 30 percent DEET is usually enough to deter the swarm and maintain sanity.

10 Mount Arab

A short, kid-friendly hike to a restored fire tower and fire watcher's cabin, with lake views in every direction.

Total distance: 2.0 miles
Type of hike: Out and back
Highest point: 2,533 feet
Vertical gain: 760 feet
Approximate hiking time: 2.5 hours

Canine compatibility: Dogs should be on leash. Bring water for your dog. Do not allow your dog on the fire tower!
Map: USGS Piercefield Quad

Finding the Trailhead: In Tupper Lake, from the junction of NY 3 and NY 30, take NY 3 west for 6.8 miles to Piercefield. Turn left in Piercefield on St. Lawrence CR 62, following the sign to Conifer and Mount Arab (the hamlets). Go 1.7 miles. Turn left on Mount Arab Road. Go 0.8 mile to the trailhead, on the left. Trailhead parking is on the right. Trailhead GPS: N44 12.819' / W74 35.754'

The Hike

Mount Arab is a perfect hike for young children and other inexperienced hikers. There is a big reward—climbing the fire tower—for relatively little effort, as the rate of ascent ranges from hardly detectable to moderate. One eight-year-old rated the hike a 9 out of 10, deducting one point because he got a couple of bug bites and because there were a few slippery spots.

The trail begins on a state conservation easement called the Conifer Easement Lands. Following the red NYSDEC markers, the smooth path heads up a steady incline through a mixed hardwood forest. The undergrowth is lush, with grass, ferns, and various shrubs, including wild raspberries, under the airy canopy. At 0.3 mile, the incline mellows as it crosses into the Adirondack Preserve. Don't be startled if you flush a grouse while walking through this classic upland habitat.

The route soon turns uphill again, though nothing extreme, as it crosses intermittent lengths of slab. In late spring, trillium poke their tri-petalled flowers toward the sky along this section of trail. The path continues to climb, helped by rock steps. The trail is older and more worn in this area, but the footing is still good and soon becomes smooth again as you head up a steeper section of the slope.

At 0.5 mile, the trail crosses a small shoulder of the mountain where grass grows along the side of the trail. The canopy, though not clear to the sky, is more open here, and there are berry bushes, so beware of prickers.

The trees soon thicken again, but not enough to block a glimpse of neighboring Wheeler, Buck, and Haystack Mountains to the left (southwest) just before you cross a wet area on lengths of puncheon.

At about 0.7 mile, the trail climbs moderately, passing a rock outcropping, which forms a pretty, moss-covered wall on your left. Then the trail flattens as it goes around a low rock wall.

The trail makes a half-circle to the northeast before bending to the right, returning to its original southeasterly direction.

At 0.9 mile, the trail heads up a rise and comes to a short steep section of slab. You can either go up the slab or take one of the switchback, to the left or right, around it. The summit is just beyond at 1.0 mile.

The fire tower stands atop the high point of the rock slab, the result of forest fires many years ago. It was in disrepair

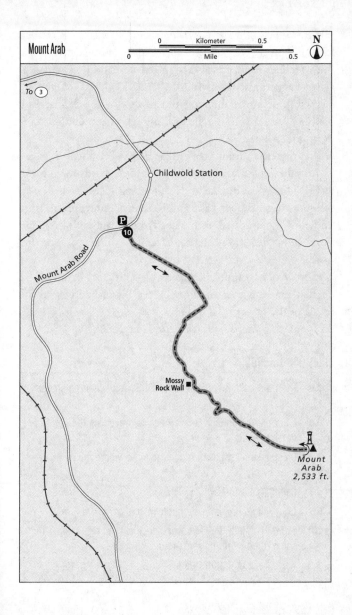

Mount Arab

To (3)

Childwold Station

P
10

Mount Arab Road

Mossy
Rock Wall

Mount
Arab
2,533 ft.

N

0   Kilometer   0.5
0   Mile   0.5

for a number of years until the Friends of Mount Arab, a local nonprofit organization, restored it. More recently, the fire watcher's cabin has also been restored and now serves as a two-room museum giving the history of Arab Mountain, background information on fire towers in the Adirondack Park and a peek into the life of those who manned the tower during its heyday.

Though the summit clearing is hemmed in by red spruce and mountain ash, there is a 360-degree view from atop the tower. Mount Arab Lake and Eagle Crag Lake are below to the southwest. Tupper Lake and Raquette Pond are the large bodies of water dotted with islands to the east, with the High Peaks beyond in the distance. Mount Matumbla stands due north.

The true summit marked by a USGS benchmark—a circular brass disc—is on an open flat bit of bedrock to the north of the tower.

Return to the trailhead by the same route.

Miles and Directions

0.0 From the trailhead, follow red NYSDEC markers up a smooth rise.

0.3 Enter the Adirondack Forest Preserve, traversing through upland forest.

0.5 Cross a small shoulder of the mountain where the canopy thins briefly.

0.7 Climb past a mossy rock wall.

0.9 Go up or go around a short, steep slab of rock.

1.0 SUMMIT! Climb the fire tower, check out the fire watcher's cabin, then return by same route.

2.0 Arrive back at the trailhead.

11 Lyon Mountain

A woodland stroll, then a fun scramble up rocks to a fire tower and an open summit with views into Canada, Vermont, and the High Peaks region of the Adirondacks.

Total distance: 6.4 miles
Type of hike: Out and back
Highest point: 3,829 feet
Vertical gain: 1,904 feet
Approximate hiking time: 5 hours

Canine compatibility: Dog-friendly. Do not allow your dog on the fire tower!
Map: USGS Lyon Mountain Quad

Finding the Trailhead: From the junction of NY 374 and Standish Road in the hamlet of Lyon Mountain, take NY 374 east for 3.6 miles. Turn right (south) on Chazy Lake Road. Go 1.7 miles. Turn right on a seasonal dirt road (formerly called Lowenburg Road) at the NYSDEC sign for Lyon Mountain. Go 0.9 mile to the end of the road. The trailhead is on the left, a continuation of the dirt road. Parking is on the right. Trailhead GPS: N44 43.424' / W73 50.519'

The Hike

Lyon Mountain is only 171 feet short of making the 4,000-footer list. It is a monadnock—a peak that stands alone, about 30 miles west of Plattsburgh, crowning the southwestern shore of Chazy Lake. From 1870 to 1967, iron ore was mined from the mountain. Considered some of the finest iron ore in the world, it was used in structures such as the Golden Gate Bridge in San Francisco. Nine years after the mine opened, Verplanck Colvin located the headquarters for his Adirondack survey at Lyon Mountain (the hamlet at the base of the mountain). In 2005 the state of New York purchased 20,000 acres of land in the northern Adirondacks, including Lyon Mountain, from the Nature Conservancy for $9.8 million, which was about the time that restoration work on the fire tower began.

Though the trail up Lyon Mountain is longer than 6 miles round-trip, it feels easier to hike than many ascents of lesser mileage. The route up Lyon Mountain was cut in 2009. Unlike most Adirondack trails, it has lots of modern-day switchbacks and a moderate incline until it meets the original trail just below the summit. Your heart will pound as you scramble up the upper slopes. But it's a worthwhile effort. The panorama from atop Lyon Mountain is the king of views in the northern Adirondacks. You can see the highest peaks in both New York and Vermont from atop its fire tower as well as Montreal, Quebec, on a clear day.

From the parking lot, continue up the dirt road on foot. It immediately turns to large uneven cobblestones, climbing gently. The route (red NYSDEC markers) is a wide, unmaintained jeep road that rises through a hardwood forest with both paper and yellow birch and striped maple in the mix. At 0.3 mile, the trail splits briefly around a stand of paper birch, then comes to a pile of sticks and logs blocking the old trail. Turn left at the sign onto the newer route, crossing a stream on a footbridge.

The trail is soft and can be muddy after a rainstorm but easygoing. It continues to climb moderately, around a long switchback and then traverses to the southwest. It's striking how different this trail is from older trails in the Adirondacks, which take a direct line up a mountain.

The trail bends left as it rounds another switchback and levels off on a lazy arc to the right. But it soon resumes S-ing through the ferns and forest, heading to the southwest.

After a slight downhill, it skirts a hillside, passing by mature hemlocks. After one particularly muddy section, stepping stones aid the climb. At 0.7 mile, the trail dips again, crossing a stream on a second footbridge. The ascent resumes, though moderately and at the same angle to the southwest.

At 1.0 mile, you cross the first lengths of slab. The trail bends right, still climbing moderately. After another long switchback, the trail zigzags through the forest. The canopy opens briefly as you wind through a small clearing of ferns. Then it heads downhill past a large glacial erratic on the right side of the trail. This huge boulder has a cleft in its side, creating a shallow overhang.

The downhill is thankfully short, then the trail levels off, passing over a small freshet. After a couple of switchbacks, it ascends more persistently, heading to the southwest. It bends to the north, passing through a grove of birch and ferns, and soon enters the lower boreal. Hemlocks and paper birch take over the forest mix.

As you pass through more switchbacks, your elevation gain becomes more evident as you begin to see sky through the trees on your left, rather than just above the treetops. The trail passes a moss-topped boulder, which forms a short wall next to the trail on a longish traverse, and then comes to the junction with the old route at 2.5 miles. Turn left, heading up the broad, washed-out trail.

The trail is steep and heads directly up the side of the mountain. It's eroded and uneven, with exposed roots winding across the path among the rocks. Indian pipe, asters, and clintonia peak up from among the rocks and roots.

At 2.7 miles, the trail passes the remains of the small fire-watcher's cabin, of which only two front steps, two footings, and the foundation wall on the uphill side remain. Beyond the cabin site the eroded, braided trail continues its persistent ascent up the steepest section yet. It's also the wettest and muddiest section after a rainstorm, but the view of Chazy Lake, which starts to appear behind you to the northeast, helps keep enthusiasm high for reaching the summit.

At 2.8 miles, the steep pitch begins to mellow. There are more sections of slab underfoot and rocks to scramble up and over. Then the fire tower suddenly appears ahead of you, looming over the treetops at 3.2 miles.

The 35-foot tower sits on open bedrock on the broad summit. It was built in 1917 and served until 1988. There is a 360-degree view, but the eastern panorama, which includes Lake Champlain, plus Mount Mansfield and Camel's Hump across the water in Vermont, draws the eye the most. The High Peaks crown the horizon to the south. Chazy Lake is the large, close body of water to the northeast. The white windmills that dot the countryside to the north produce electricity for the surrounding communities. After looking around, descend the tower and head toward the lake view, where there are open ledges and several perfect picnic spots. The view is much better here than on the west side of the summit, which is covered with thin, scrubby trees.

Return to the trailhead by the same route.

Miles and Directions

0.0 Trailhead. Head up the unmaintained jeep road.

0.3 Turn left onto the newer route, crossing a stream on a footbridge.

0.7 Dip down to a second footbridge over another stream.

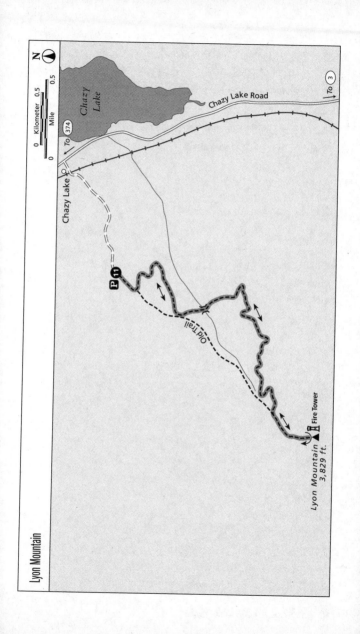

Lyon Mountain

N

0 Kilometer 0.5

0 Mile 0.5

Chazy Lake

Chazy Lake Road

To 374

To 3

Chazy Lake

P 11

Old Trail

Lyon Mountain
3,829 ft.

Fire Tower

1.0 Pass over slab where fallen trees have peeled the soil away.

2.5 Turn left at the junction with the old route, climbing the wide, washed-out trail.

2.7 Pass the remains of the fire-watcher's cabin.

2.8 The pitch mellows.

3.2 FIRE TOWER! Return by the same route.

6.4 Arrive back at the trailhead.

12 Saint Regis Mountain

A relatively easy hike, considering the mileage, to a restored fire tower and a fantastic view of the Saint Regis Canoe Area.

Total distance: 6.6 miles
Type of hike: Out and back
Highest point: 2,858 feet
Vertical gain: 1,260 feet
Approximate hiking time: 5.5 hours

Canine compatibility: Dog-friendly. Dogs should not climb the tower.
Map: USGS Saint Regis Mountain Quad

Finding the Trailhead: At the junction of NY 86 and NY 30 in Paul Smiths, turn right (north) on NY 30. Go 100 yards, then turn left (west) on Keese Mills Road. Go 2.5 miles. The trailhead parking lot is on the left side of the road just past the turn for Topridge Road. Walk 0.1 mile down Topridge Road to the trailhead. Trailhead GPS: N44 25.923' / W74 18.011'

The Hike

Saint Regis Mountain is a short hike if you take a boat across Upper Saint Regis Lake, but if you must go by car, you'll need to follow the full route, which is described here. It's over 6 miles, but it's easy terrain-wise, as most of the route is the approach to the mountain, not the ascent. And it's very pretty, especially when the leaves reach their peak color in the fall (late September here) due to the many maples in the forest mix. There's a fantastic view from the summit plateau, whether you climb the fire tower or not. Although on the long side for young children, this is a great hike for older kids and dogs.

From the parking lot on Keese Mills Road, cross over the metal bridge on foot and walk the 0.1 mile down the dirt road to the trailhead, which is on the right. From the sign-in box, cross a streamlet on a long footbridge and climb a few stone steps following the red NYSDEC markers. The trail bends left (south) and continues to climb moderately up the small hillside. It quickly flattens out and then dips past a small grassy wetland on your left. The footing is smooth as you wind through the classic mixed northern forest.

At 0.2 mile (from the trailhead), the trail swings right (northwest) on another easy, short climb and then levels off on a woods road. A moment later watch for a short detour over a large low boulder. The woods road goes straight, but it's blocked by sticks. The trail merges with the road again on the other side of the elongated boulder and then narrows to a footpath over a length of slab as it continues deeper into the forest, climbing moderately.

At 0.8 mile, the path passes through a grove of mature hemlocks where the ground is clear of flora and debris except for a soft carpet of duff. Then the trail begins a long, gradual downhill and hardwoods return to the mix. Eventually the path bends to the south on a sustained undulating traverse.

At 2 miles, the trail crosses a footbridge over a pretty streamlet and bends to the southwest. Soon afterward it finally begins to climb the mountain. Though a steady pitch, the footing is smooth and not overly strenuous. After a dip, the climb resumes, now with roots and stones strewn along the path.

At 2.4 miles, the trail climbs more persistently up through a young forest onto the shoulder of the mountain. A few stone steps aid the ascent.

At 2.6 miles, the trail bends northwest up a much longer stone staircase and then more stone steps just beyond a low, mossy rock outcropping. Look back to glimpse Spitfire Lake through the trees. You notice the elevation gain as the forest brightens and the canopy thins.

The ascent is direct, passing under another low rock wall, and then heads up through a well-traveled, eroded section. After scrambling over a rock jumble, the ascent eases on a small high shelf before winding around the north side of the mountain.

At 3.1 miles, a spur trail on the right leads to a view to the west and north. The fire tower is just above you at 3.3 miles.

The 35-foot tall tower was erected in 1910, then closed in 1990, one of the last manned towers in the Adirondacks. For many years, the state of New York intended to remove the tower because it was considered a nonconforming structure in a wilderness area, but it was also listed on the registry for National Historic Places. The Friends of Saint Regis Mountain Fire Tower collected over 2,500 signatures, successfully petitioning the state to allow the tower to be restored for the enjoyment of hikers. In 2016, renovations to the tower were completed, and it is once again open. Whether you climb to the tower's observation cabin or relax on the broad expanse of rock below it, you'll love the unobstructed view of the 19,000-acre Saint Regis Canoe Area, the largest wilderness canoe area in the northeastern United States and the only one in New York.

Return to the trailhead by the same route.

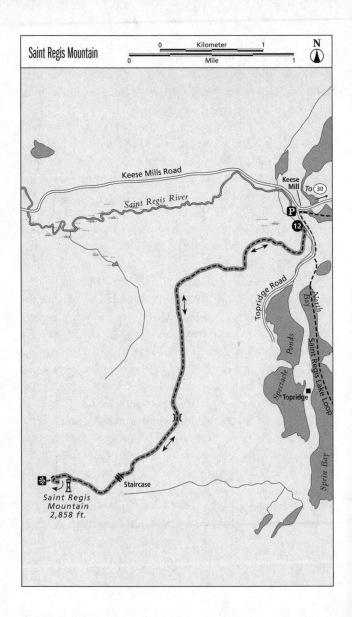

Saint Regis Mountain

	Kilometer		
0			1
0	Mile		1

N

Keese Mills Road

Saint Regis River

Keese
Mill

To 30

P

12

Topridge Road

Spectacle
Ponds

Topridge

North
Bay

Saint Regis Lake Loop

Spitfire Bay

Staircase

Saint Regis
Mountain
2,858 ft.

Miles and Directions

0.0 Trailhead. Enter the woods on a footbridge.

0.2 Swing right and climb a short way to a woods road.

0.8 Pass through a grove of tall hemlocks.

2.0 Cross a footbridge and begin climbing.

2.4 Reach a shoulder of the mountain.

2.6 Continue the steep ascent aided by stone steps.

3.1 Turn right onto a short spur to a rock outcropping just below the summit for a view to the north and west.

3.3 SUMMIT! Return by the same route.

6.6 Arrive back at the trailhead. Walk the short way down Topridge Road back to your car.

Central Region

The Central Adirondacks lie at the geographic heart of the Adirondack Park. Two United States Presidents have visited this region. In 1892, Grover Cleveland, no longer in office, visited a famous local guide named Alvah Dunning on the edge of Blue Mountain Lake. In 1901, Theodore Roosevelt was near North Creek when he received word that President McKinley had died and that he was now President of the United States. Among the other famous people to visit area, Thomas Edison used to spend his summers in Blue Mountain Lake, where he wired a local hotel called Prospect House, making it the first hotel in the world to have electricity.

While the mountains of the Central Adirondacks are under the lorded 4,000-foot mark, there are a number of bald summits or fire towers with 360-degree views. Though the region was heavily logged, the forests have grown back and are now rich with wildflowers and wildlife. Indian Lake lies near the center of the region, but there are dozens of other lakes and ponds, 36 in the Siamese Ponds Wilderness alone. Several well-known rivers, including the Hudson and the East Branch Sacandaga Rivers, also flow through the area.

13 Goodnow Mountain

A modest hike along a nature trail to a 60-foot fire tower with breathtaking views of the surrounding mountains, lakes, and ponds.

Total distance: 4.0 miles
Type of hike: Out and back
Highest point: 2,664 feet
Vertical gain: 1,035 feet
Approximate hiking time: 3 hours

Canine compatibility: Dog-friendly. Dogs should be on leash. Do not allow dogs up on the fire tower!
Map: USGS Newcomb Quad

Finding the Trailhead: At the junction of NY 30 and NY 28N in Long Lake, travel east on NY 28N toward Newcomb for 11.0 miles. Turn right at the white sign for Goodnow Mountain (not a NYSDEC sign) to find the trailhead and parking area. *Note:* Goodnow Mountain is a day-use area. It is open daily from sunrise to sunset. Trailhead GPS: N43 58.178' / W74 12.864'

The Hike

Named for Sylvester Goodnow, a homesteader who settled at the base of the mountain in the 1820s, Goodnow Mountain is the only hike in this book that is not maintained by the NYSDEC, though the state built the fire tower on its summit. The mountain is located in the Huntington Wildlife Forest, which is owned by the State University of New York (SUNY) College of Environmental Science and Forestry in Syracuse. The forest is a field station for wildlife research and ecology studies. The trail is maintained jointly by SUNY and the Town of Newcomb. Camping, hunting, and plant collecting are not allowed.

From the trailhead, follow the orange markers with black arrows into the woods. As you climb, you also pass by yellow numbered markers that denote stations on the nature trail up the mountain. Look for a brochure inside the sign-in box to help you interpret each point.

The wide trail climbs moderately from the sign-in box up a couple of log ties and then comes almost immediately to a highly constructed wooden staircase with a handrail. It bends right (north) and flattens, crossing a wet area. At 0.1 mile, it passes over a streamlet on a bog bridge, heads downhill, and crosses another length of puncheon before resuming the climb.

The smooth trail rolls past towering beech, birch, maple, and hemlock. At 0.6 mile, the trail turns upward over railroad-tie steps and another bog bridge. Partway up the slope a mature yellow birch grows atop a large rock. Its roots sprawl down the sides of the rock like a giant octopus reaching its tentacles toward the ground.

After passing a bench, the climb becomes more persistent but mellows ten minutes later as it bends to the right (south). At 1.4 miles, the trail bends left (north), then ascends up a long length of slab. It traverses a long arcing bog bridge and then comes to the foundation of a cabin. A short spur leads to an old well.

After passing the remains of another old cabin, it crosses a long length of puncheon, then ascends in waves toward the summit. Evergreens take over the forest mix as you sense the elevation gain.

The trail narrows and feels like a long skinny terrace on the side of the mountain. At 1.8 miles, you pass another

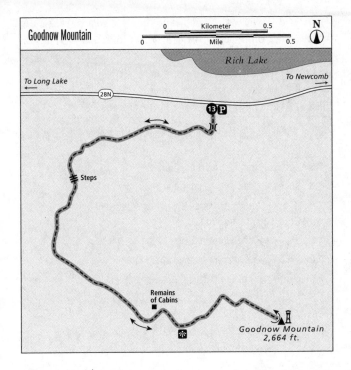

Kilometer
0 0.5
Mile
0 0.5

N

Rich Lake

To Long Lake
←

To Newcomb
→

28N

13 P

Steps

Remains
of Cabins

Goodnow Mountain
2,664 ft.

bench, this one with a view of the hills to the southwest. The trail dips off this high shoulder of the mountain, then continues through conifers, climbing moderately. *Note:* Some of the trail markers are now red NYSDEC markers.

After crossing several lengths of slab, you arrive at the fire tower at 2.0 miles. The tower is enclosed, providing welcome protection from the elements and the bugs. The names of the fire-watchers who were stationed here during the tower's working life, from 1922 to 1979, are inscribed on the map inside the high cabin. The circular map helps you navigate around the panorama, which includes Rich Lake that is below you to the north; and the Seward and Santanoni Ranges, Algonquin Peak, and Mounts Colden and Marcy in the distance.

Return by the same route.

Miles and Directions

0.0 Climb up log ties and a wood staircase just above the sign-in box.

0.1 Cross a streamlet on a bog bridge.

0.6 Climb upward over railroad-tie steps.

1.4 The trail bends left. Pass the remains of two cabins on long stretches of puncheon.

1.8 Pause at a bench with a view to the southwest.

2.0 FIRE TOWER! Return by the same route.

4.0 Arrive back at the trailhead and parking area.

14 Blue Mountain

One of the most popular hikes in the Adirondacks, up a nature trail to a fire tower and a 360-degree view.

Total distance: 4.0 miles
Type of hike: Out and back
Highest point: 3,750 feet
Vertical gain: 1,537 feet
Approximate hiking time: 4 hours

Canine compatibility: Dog-friendly. Dogs should be on leash. Do not allow dogs on the fire tower!
Map: USGS Blue Mountain Quad

Finding the Trailhead: From the junction of NY 28, NY 28N, and NY 30 in the hamlet of Blue Mountain Lake, go 1.4 miles north on NY 28N/NY 30. The trailhead and parking area are on the right (east) side of the road at the top of the hill just beyond the Adirondack Museum. Trailhead GPS: N43 52.475' / W74 25.851'

The Hike

Blue Mountain is one of the most climbed mountains in the Adirondack Park. About 15,000 people ascend to its fire tower along a fourteen-point nature trail each year. If you follow the trail guide available at the sign-in box, over the course of the hike, you get a good sense of the geologic and natural history of the region. Some of the numbered points of the nature trail are included as markers in this trail description.

The route up Blue Mountain (red NYSDEC markers) shares a trailhead with the route to Tirrell Pond (yellow markers). The smooth, flat trail enters the woods, then swings right, just as a smaller footpath from the right joins the main path at a second sign-in box for the nature trail. The path up the mountain begins as a woods road, heading east and climbing gently.

At 0.3 mile, the trail passes a "2" on a tree, a marker for the nature trail where a balsam fir grows atop a rock. It crosses a wet area on puncheon steps, then narrows to a footpath, though the path is still obvious and well used.

As you climb through the mixed northern forest, the maples become fewer and the birch and hemlock increase. Painted trillium, hobblebush and clintonia bloom beside the trail in early June. The trail flattens as you pass a mature paper birch (#4 on the nature trail), then traverse more lengths of puncheon. At 0.8 mile, you cross a pretty stream flowing over some slab (#5), the water from which will eventually end up in the Atlantic Ocean.

Beyond the stream the path gets steeper. Rock steps aid the ascent as the canopy gets thinner above. Then the trail heads downhill briefly, crossing more puncheon, as you pass #7 amidst a stand of paper birch.

After crossing two streamlets the trail climbs again. At 1.2 miles, it swings east toward a rise of land, then ascends some rubble and slab. The climb is now more sustained, the real climb up the mountain. Spruce and other conifers take over the forest mix. The trail is worn to bedrock for most of the steady, steep ascent, which can be slippery if wet.

The grade eases at 1.8 miles (#13) as you near the summit area, winding through stunted evergreens.

At 2.0 miles, you reach the broad grassy clearing and the fire tower at the top of the mountain. The concrete slabs near the tower are all that remains of the former fire-watcher's cabin.

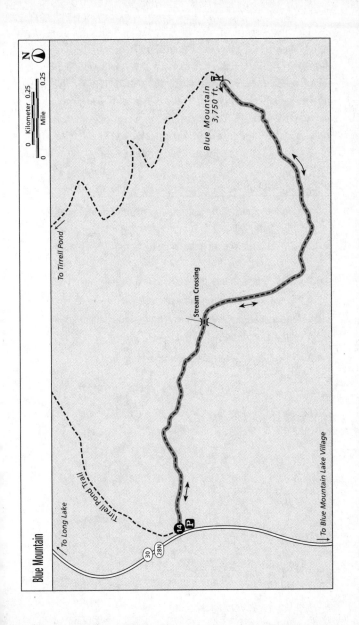

Blue Mountain

To Tirrell Pond

Blue Mountain
3,750 ft.

Stream Crossing

Tirrell Pond Trail

To Long Lake

30 28N

14 P

To Blue Mountain Lake Village

N

0   Kilometer   0.25

0   Mile   0.25

The view from the tower is an Adirondack favorite, with Blue Mountain Lake and Raquette Lake to the west and the High Peaks on the horizon to the northeast. Snowy and Wakely Mountains, both with fire towers, lie to the south. But more impressive than the peaks is the amount of water all around you. There seems more water than land as you gaze across this region of Adirondacks.

Return to the trailhead by the same route.

Miles and Directions

0.0 From the trailhead, follow the red NYSDEC markers toward Blue Mountain.

0.3 Pass a balsam fir tree growing atop a rock (#2 on the nature trail).

0.8 Cross a stream flowing over slab (#5 on the nature trail).

1.2 Swing east and begin the real climb.

1.8 The trail eases as you approach the summit plateau.

2.0 FIRE TOWER! Return by the same route.

4.0 Arrive back at the trailhead and parking area.

Southern Region

The Southern Adirondacks encompass the section of the Adirondack Park south of NY 8 between Prospect and Speculator, plus the land in the southern half of the Wilcox Lake Wild Forest between Speculator and Lake George village. This is the region closest to large population centers, particularly Albany, the state capital, yet the trails are not crowded, especially midweek.

The southern region is best characterized by braided rivers and creeks that wind their way between the lakes and ponds that dot the hilly countryside. The Silver Lake Wilderness is the only designated wilderness area in the region. Most of the backcountry is contained in Ferris Lake Wild Forest, Shaker Mountain Wild Forest, and Wilcox Wild Forest.

Because the topography of the Southern Adirondacks is gentler than in the heart of the Adirondack Park, the hikes here are particularly nice for families who are either new to hiking or who don't want to make a full day of it. The routes described here are among the classics of the region. Each offers a beautiful view at the end of a pleasant woodland walk, with just enough topography to keep things interesting.

15   Crane Mountain-Crane Pond Loop

A fun climb up rocks, slab, and a couple of ladders to an eye-popping view of the region, then a gentle descent to a small remote pond.

Total distance: 3.1 miles
Type of hike: Lollipop
Highest point: 2,851 feet
Vertical gain: 1,387 feet
Approximate hiking time: 3 hours

Canine compatibility: Not dog-friendly due to ladders near summit
Map: USGS Johnsburg Quad

Finding the Trailhead: At the junction of US 9 and NY 418 in Warrensburg, go 3.6 miles west on NY 418 toward Thurman. At a cluster of signs on the right, turn right (northwest) on Athol Road, following the signs toward the town hall and Veteran's Field. Go 1.1 miles to a T. Turn right (northeast) onto Cameron Road. Go 0.9 mile, then bear right (north) on Glen/Athol Road. Go 1.4 miles, then turn left on Valley Road. Go 4.6 miles, then turn left on Garnet Lake Road South. Go 1.3 miles, then turn right on Ski Hi Road (dirt). Go 1.9 miles. The road narrows at the top of a hill as it crosses onto forest preserve land. The road winds through a wetland and ends at the trailhead parking area. Trailhead GPS: N43 32.239' / W73 58.034'

The Hike

The hardest part of this hike is finding the trailhead, but once there you'll enjoy this interesting climb to the summit of Crane Mountain and the pleasant walk to the pond of the same name. This hike is a lollipop, meaning you begin and end on the same trail, but make a loop over the mountaintop, then down to the pond on a high shelf of the mountain, before rejoining the trail you started on.

There are two stories behind the name of the mountain and the pond, one crediting a pair of cranes that were rumored to have nested on the pond in the previous century, the other crediting a state surveyor with the last name of Crane who marked a 55-mile line that ran over the mountaintop.

Two trails depart from the sign-in box, one to Putnam Farm Junction/Crane Pond and the other to Crane Mountain/Crane Pond. *Note:* The actual name of the pond is "Crane Mountain Pond," though the sign says only CRANE POND. Bear right (north), following the red NYSDEC markers toward Crane Mountain. The well-worn trail tilts upward over rocks and roots through a dense hardwood forest of maple, birch, and beech. The footing soon becomes a jumble of rocks as you quickly gain elevation.

You can see the neighboring hills through the trees where the trail bends left (northwest) at the base of a sizable rock face. The jumble of rocks becomes more vertical as you climb up the broad rocky slope, similar to ascending an old slide, but more stable.

At 0.5 mile, at the top of the talus, a yellow arrow points to the right up a section of smooth slab, a low-angle friction climb. At the top of the slab, there is a short spur trail to a lookout to the northwest over blueberry bushes. Crane Mountain is a wild-blueberry bonanza in July.

Above the slab, the forest transitions to birch and softwoods, and the trail changes to roots underfoot. It parallels a ledge, passing a few other spots where you can poke through to get a view. Then the trail breaks out onto an expanse of slab, part of the patchwork of rock that you can see from the road as you approach the mountain.

Head straight up the slab to the junction where the Summit Trail and the Pond Trail split. Bear right (northeast) on the Summit Trail. The path dips, then heads up another short, steep, eroded jumble of rocks and roots before reaching better footing.

At 0.8 mile, a short ladder aids the ascent up a short rock wall, then the trail flattens through a grove of hemlocks as it bends to the east.

At 1.2 miles, the trail swings back to the north up another washout, then climbs more rubble to a second, longer 24-rung ladder. Above the ladder there is an excellent view from a rocky perch to the southwest. Wildlands sprawl before you as far as you can see! From here, the trail winds up a few more steps, arriving at the summit at 1.4 miles.

The footings of an old fire tower are embedded in the rock on the summit, but there is no need for a tower to take in the incredible view. The mountains along Lake George and the Green Mountains of Vermont beyond lie to the east. Moose Mountain and Baldhead dominate the view to the south, and Blue Mountain stands guard on the far shore of Garnet Lake to the southwest.

From the summit, head north on the elongated summit ledge, which narrows to a footpath. The path begins with a gentle downhill traverse, then descends more deliberately. The trail is well used but less rocky than on the way up. It levels off as you reenter the hardwoods, becoming narrower and smoother. At 1.9 miles, it passes through a short muddy stretch just before arriving at the eastern side of Crane Mountain Pond. Look for a short spur on your right for a peek across the fourteen-acre pond.

The trail bends to the west, following a yellow arrow and heading along the southern shore of the pond. You can see

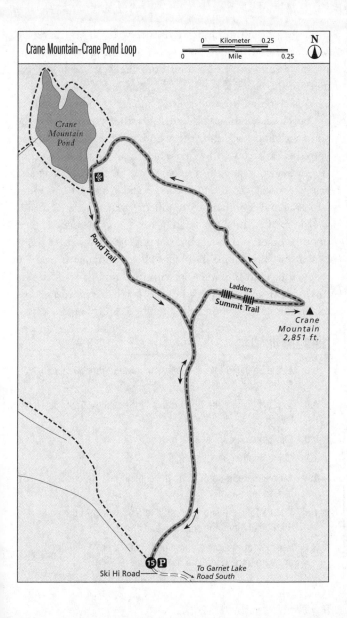

Crane Mountain–Crane Pond Loop

0   Kilometer   0.25

0   Mile   0.25

N

Crane Mountain Pond

Pond Trail

Ladders
Summit Trail

Crane
Mountain
2,851 ft.

Ski Hi Road

15 P

To Garnet Lake
Road South

a nice beach and campsite across the water. If you have the time, the beach is a pleasant spot for a swim. You may see anglers casting for brook trout from the shore or from float tubes in the water.

At 2.1 miles, the trail splits. The right fork takes you to the beach and campsite. Bear left (southeast), away from the pond, heading back into the woods on the Pond Trail (no sign). It's easy to walk by this junction as the pond continually draws your attention. If you miss it, the next left also brings you back to the trailhead via the Putnam Farm Junction Trail, but it adds an extra mile to your hike.

The trail climbs moderately on a dry streambed, then smooths out. It crosses a length of puncheon through a hemlock grove, traversing a shoulder of the mountain, then, at 2.6 miles, you reach the junction with the Summit Trail, closing the loop. Bear right, retracing the last half mile down the rocky hillside, returning to the trailhead at 3.1 miles.

Miles and Directions

0.0   At the trailhead take the right trail toward Crane Mountain/ Crane Pond.

0.5   Turn right where the Pond Trail and the Summit Trail split, following the Summit Trail.

0.8   Climb a ladder up a short rock wall.

1.2   Climb another, longer ladder.

1.4   SUMMIT! Head north along the summit ridge to descend toward the pond.

1.9   POND! Take the short spur trail for a view across the pond, then head along the southern shore of the pond.

2.1   Bear left at the fork on the Pond Trail (no sign), heading away from the pond into the woods.

2.6 Close the loop at the junction with the Summit Trail. Turn right and retrace back to the trailhead.

3.1 Arrive back at the trailhead and parking area.

16 Echo Cliff

A short, steep ascent to a cliff-top view of Piseco Lake and the Silver Lake Wilderness.

Total distance: 1.6 miles
Type of hike: Out and back
Highest point: 2,435 feet
Vertical gain: 651 feet
Approximate hiking time: 1.5 hours

Canine compatibility: Dog-friendly. Dogs should be on leash around cliff.

Map: USGS Piseco Lake Quad

Finding the trailhead: From US 8 at the southwestern corner of Piseco Lake, turn north on West Shore Road (aka Old Piseco Road). *Note:* The road sign may be missing, but follow the brown and gold NYSDEC sign at the turn that says POINT COMFORT, LITTLE SAND POINT, POPLAR POINT, PISECO VILLAGE. Go 2.5 miles to the trailhead for Panther Mountain on the left (west) side of the road. Trailhead parking is a turnout on the right (east) side of the road, across from the trailhead. Trailhead GPS: N43 24.683' / W74 33.448'

The Hike

Echo Cliff is a rock outcropping on the eastern side of Panther Mountain. The summit of the mountain is another 300 vertical feet higher than the cliff, but it is covered with trees and offers little view. The cliff is the better destination, a perfect hike if you want little exercise and a big reward.

From the trailhead, follow the blue NYSDEC markers up the wide, well-used path into a hardwood forest. The hike begins on a gentle incline through maple, beech, and birch,

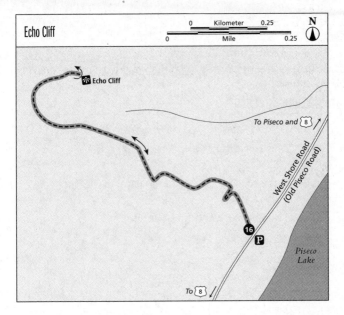

but soon becomes more persistent as it passes over a section of slab.

At 0.4 mile, the trail bends to the right (north) and eases briefly, becoming a smooth, wide but normal footpath, unlike the superhighway below.

It eases again at 0.5 mile, as you cross a small shoulder of the mountain. After passing a square, flat-top boulder on your left, the trail heads upward again, bending to the northeast through scattered rocks and boulders. It climbs along a low cliff, then, as the cliff peters out, the trail turns steep, rough, and rocky.

You can glimpse Piseco Lake through the trees on your right just before a short scramble up some rock and the exposed roots of a large hemlock. The cliff is just above the hemlock at 0.8 mile.

The view from this lofty perch is an eastern panorama, with Piseco Lake immediately below you, and smaller Spy Lake just beyond to the southeast.

Return to the trailhead by the same route.

Miles and Directions

0.0 Begin at the trailhead on the west side of Piseco Lake.

0.4 The route bends to the right, becoming smooth and more like a footpath.

0.5 Cross a small shoulder of the mountain. The trail then turns steep and rocky.

0.8 ECHO CLIFF! Return by the same route.

1.6 Arrive back at the trailhead.

17 Hadley Mountain

A family-friendly hike to a restored fire tower and an expansive 360-degree view that includes the High Peaks, the Green Mountains (Vermont), and the Berkshires (Massachusetts) on a clear day.

Total distance: 3.2 miles
Type of hike: Out and back
Highest point: 2,648 feet
Vertical gain: 1,500 feet
Approximate hiking time: 3.5 hours

Canine compatibility: Dog-friendly. Do not allow dogs on the fire tower!
Maps: USGS Stony Creek Quad (summit), Conklingville Quad (trailhead)

Finding the trailhead: At the town hall in the center of Hadley, go 3.0 miles north on Stony Creek Road (also called Saratoga CR 1). Turn left (northwest) on Hadley Hill Road. Go 4.3 miles, then turn right (north) on Tower Road (dirt). Go 1.4 miles to the trailhead, which is on the left (west) side of the road. Trailhead GPS: N43 22.447' / W73 57.048'

The Hike

Located in the Wilcox Lake Wild Forest, a 140,000-acre forest preserve, Hadley Mountain is the highest point at the southern end of West Mountain, a half-mile-long ridge. It is a favorite hike in the Saratoga area for the views from its fire tower, which was placed on the National Register of Historic Places in 2001. While modest in terms of mileage, it is a persistent climb.

From the trailhead, follow the red NYSDEC markers up the broad, rocky trail. It begins on a moderate slope through a mixed northern forest. Log steps cross sections of slab to help hold small vestiges of soil on the well-trodden path.

By 0.5 mile, the trail becomes predominantly slab as you climb steadily upward. The slab is smooth underfoot, but use caution as it can be slick when wet. As you gain elevation, ironically fewer evergreens grow in the airy, bright forest, which becomes predominantly birch and maple.

The trail winds around several elongated switchbacks, then resumes its uphill climb in its original westerly direction. Broad-leaf wild raspberries and jewelweed bloom beside the path in early August.

At 0.8 mile, it reaches a plateau and bends to the right (north). Though the trees remain tall, your surroundings feel more open and grassy, with wood asters, black raspberries, and goldenrod coloring the woods around you.

The trail climbs a short, pebbly rise, passing a large boulder with a tree growing on its top.

Minutes later, at 1.3 miles, a yellow arrow points the direction (left) at a sharp bend in the trail.

The ascent continues on a moderate grade, still in the hardwoods, though they become shorter overhead. After another steep, uphill burst, the canopy breaks and you get your first view of Great Sacandaga Lake to the southwest. Great Sacandaga Lake is a 29-mile-long reservoir formed by a dam on the Sacandaga River at its northeast end. In the late nineteenth and early twentieth centuries, the river inundated the Albany area on several occasions, causing extensive damage. The dam has since stemmed the chance of major flooding, while creating one of the largest bodies of water within the Adirondack Park.

The trail opens onto ledges that curve around the mountain to the north. You can see Lake George to the northeast

Hadley Mountain

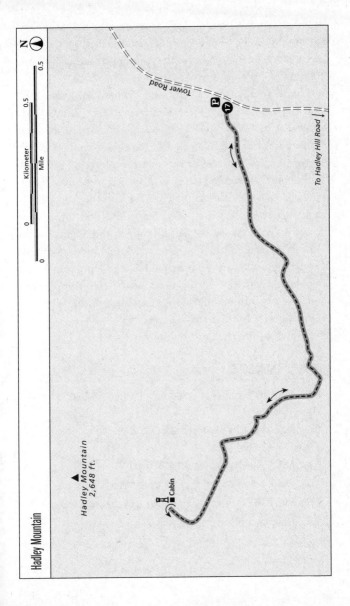

extending to the horizon before reentering the trees. The trail climbs easily to the summit plateau, passing a spur to the caretaker's cabin and reaching the fire tower just beyond at 1.6 miles.

The original fire tower atop Hadley Mountain was built in 1916 of wood. The steel tower, which stands today, replaced it in 1920. Since 1996, a summit steward has lived in the observer's cabin from July 4th through Labor Day, greeting hikers and answering questions. Hikers receive an "I climbed Hadley Mountain" card, similar to cards that fire-watchers gave out at many of the towers in the Adirondacks when they were still used to detect forest fires. From atop the tower, you can see the High Peaks to the north and the Catskills to the south. The Green Mountains in Vermont lie on the eastern horizon beyond Lake George and Lake Champlain, with the northern tip of the Berkshires to the southeast. The rolling hills of the southern Adirondacks form layers of green and blue to the west.

Return to the trailhead by the same route.

Miles and Directions

0.0 Enter the woods on a rock-strewn trail (red NYSDEC markers).

0.5 Ascend lengths of smooth slab. (**Caution:** Slab is extremely slick when wet.)

0.8 Reach a plateau and bend right (north).

1.3 Follow the yellow arrow as the trail turns sharply to the left.

1.6 FIRE TOWER! Return to the trailhead by the same route.

3.2 Arrive back at the trailhead and parking area.

18 Kane Mountain

A short, kid–friendly hike to a restored fire tower and views of the Canada Lake region.

Total distance: 1.4 miles
Type of hike: Out and back
Highest point: 2,180 feet
Vertical gain: 535 feet
Approximate hiking time: 1.5 hours

Canine compatibility: Dog-friendly. Do not allow dogs on the fire tower!
Map: USGS Canada Lake Quad

Finding the trailhead: From NY 29A in Canada Lake, turn north on Green Lake Road (dirt). Go 0.6 mile, then bear left at the parking sign on a tree to your right. Go 0.1 mile to the trailhead on your left. Parking for hikers is a pullout for 8 to 10 cars opposite the trailhead. Trailhead GPS: N43 10.852' / W74 30.303'

The Hike

Kane Mountain is a small peak on the northwestern side of Green Lake in the Shaker Mountain Wild Forest, a 40,500-acre preserve known for the southern terminus of the Northville–Lake Placid Trail, the "long trail" of the Adirondacks. Though Kane may be a minor peak, it is worth visiting the restored fire tower on its summit for a view of the Catskills to the south, the High Peaks to the north, and the many nearby lakes.

There are three approaches to the mountain, one from the north, one from the south, and a third from the east. The southern route is 0.2 mile shorter, steeper, and without a parking area for hikers. The approach from the north is not clearly marked and crosses a private campground which charges hikers a fee to pass through. The route described here is from the east. It is slightly longer than the southern route, but it is the most hiker-friendly.

The broad trail departs to the left of the sign-in box, following red NYSDEC markers. It heads northwest at first, climbing steadily on a moderate grade. While some rocks and roots litter the trail, the footing is generally good as you pass through a forest of birch, maple, poplar, and scattered hemlock.

At 0.2 mile, the trail bends to the left, heading east. It climbs a couple of short, steep sections that seem easier because of the good footing.

At 0.4 mile, you come to a small washout where the trail is worn down to bedrock. The path strays to the right for about 20 yards, where hikers have gone around the washout. It becomes more eroded as you pass through a lawn of ferns beneath the trees, then it arcs left (southwest), continuing to ascend at a moderate rate. As you traverse a longer length of slab, you sense the top of the hill.

At 0.7 miles, the trail reaches the summit, passing between the fire tower and the deserted fire-watcher's cabin. Built in 1925, the Kane Mountain fire tower was used for fire detection until 1987, then abandoned. Restored in 1993 by the Canada Lake Protective Association and NYSDEC, it was the second tower, after Goodnow Mountain, to be noted for its historical importance and rejuvenated as a hiking destination in the Adirondack Park. You'll love the breeze on a hot day and the 360-degree view, particularly of sizable Canada Lake to the south. On a windy day, eat lunch on the

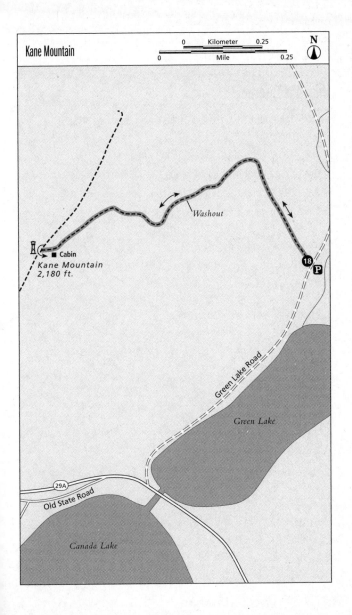

Kane Mountain

0 Kilometer 0.25
0 Mile 0.25

N

Washout

Cabin
Kane Mountain
2,180 ft.

18
P

Green Lake Road

Green Lake

29A
Old State Road

Canada Lake

flat spot just south of the cabin, which is more sheltered than the broad, exposed area around base of the tower.

Return by the same route.

Miles and Directions

0.0 Take the trail to the left of the sign-in box (red NYSDEC markers).

0.2 The trail bends to the left (southwest).

0.4 Climb a small washout where the trail is worn to bedrock.

0.7 FIRE TOWER! Return by the same route.

1.4 Arrive back at the trailhead and parking area.

West Central Region

If you are looking for solitude, you'll see few other people on the trails in the West Central Adirondacks, though there are many beautiful places to visit. There are only a couple of modest mountaintops here, but a plethora of lovely lakes, rivers, ponds, swamps, and boglands await those who venture into this peaceful part of the Adirondack Park. The region was heavily logged then ravaged by fire, but the forests have largely recovered and blanket the region with an array of northern hardwoods and conifers. While the hikes in this section are not particularly long or challenging, they will take you to special places, each with a view of water and each lovely in its own unique way.

When hiking the West Central Adirondacks, be sure to wear waterproof-breathable footwear as the routes may be wet, and bring a generous supply of bug repellent. The hikes described here are particularly appealing from late September through early October, when the leaves are aflame with color, though they are enjoyable any time of the year.

19 Bald Mountain (Rondaxe)

A kid-friendly hike, even for small children, with a number of cliff-top views en route to a fire tower.

Total distance: 2.0 miles
Type of hike: Out and back
Highest point: 2,350 feet
Vertical gain: 353 feet
Approximate hiking time: 2 hours

Canine compatibility: Dog-friendly. Do not allow dogs on the fire tower!
Map: USGS Eagle Bay Quad

Finding the Trailhead: From the Town of Webb Visitor's Center by the covered bridge in Old Forge, go 4.7 miles east on NY 28. Turn left (north) on Rondaxe Road. Go 0.1 mile. The trailhead and trailhead parking lot is on the left.

From the junction of Big Moose Road and NY 28 in Eagle Bay, go 4.6 miles west on NY 28. Turn right (north) on Rondaxe Road. Trailhead GPS: N43 44.732' / W74 54.009'

The Hike

There are sixteen Bald Mountains in New York State. This one is tagged with the suffix "Rondaxe," the name of a lake just to the north of the mountain and is sometimes called Rondaxe Mountain. However, the lakes on the other side of it are the main draw on this short hike. Bald Mountain (Rondaxe) forms an imposing ridge along the northwestern side of the Fulton Chain of lakes, which begins at Old Forge with First Lake and flows through eight lakes en route to Raquette Lake. The Fulton Chain is a popular canoe route. From Bald Mountain, you can see most of the Fulton Chain.

It is a classic short mileage/big reward hike, perfect for young children. For a modest effort, you get a number of views along the ledgy climb, then an extraordinary 360-degree view from the fire tower on the summit.

From the trailhead, follow the red NYSDEC markers into a hardwood forest on a broad path. The gentle trail is laced with just enough roots to snag a toe if you're not watching.

At 0.2 mile, the trail turns uphill over a length of slab. Stay to the right for the easiest way up the rock, then turn left near the top of the rock to stay on the official trail on top of the ridge, rather than straying into the woods straight ahead.

The trail continues upward over more roots and slab. Soon you can see Fourth Lake through the trees. At a small perch, the trail appears to go left, but bear right up the rock, staying on the ridge.

The trail levels off on slab, passing through shady woods, which cool you on a hot day. At 0.5 mile, the canopy breaks above a broader area of bedrock, as the trail passes a lookout. Again, the trail looks like it should go right in the woods, but follow the view along the cliff line. Moments later you'll get your first big view of the Fulton Chain.

Just past the overlook, the trail passes over a hump of rock then flattens, winding along the ridgeline. At 0.6 mile, it crosses a short, wide bog bridge to another opening on the ledges. Walk farther along the open rock following yellow painted blazes to another view down to the lake and to the mountains at the end of the lake to the east.

The trail continues to traverse the ridge following a rib of rock. At the next long, open break in the canopy, you can glimpse the fire tower above the treetops. Bear slightly right away from the edge of the cliff to find the fire tower straight ahead at 1.0 mile.

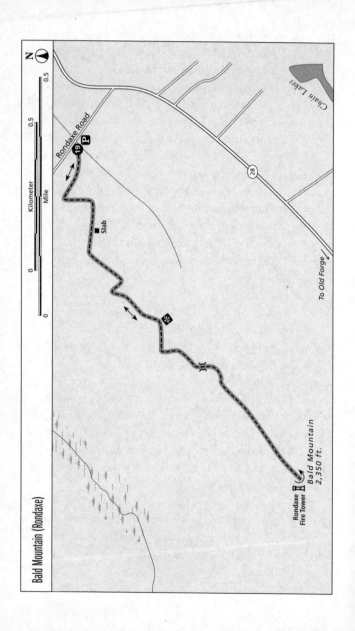

Bald Mountain (Rondaxe)

N

Kilometer
0   0.5   0.5
0   0.5
Mile

Rondaxe Road

19 P

28

Slab

To Old Forge

Chain Lakes

Rondaxe Fire Tower
Bald Mountain
2,350 ft.

Built in 1917, Rondaxe Tower was one of 120 fire towers atop peaks in New York in the early 20th century. Like other fire towers, the original one was built of wood, then later replaced with the steel structure that stands today. The fire-watcher not only looked for forest fires but also recorded all airplanes in the region during World War II. The state retired this tower from active duty in 1990. It reopened in 2005 thanks to efforts by the Friends of Bald Mountain, who maintain it for hikers.

The 360-degree view from the top of the tower is pleasing in all directions, but your eyes will be drawn to the panorama from First to Fourth Lakes below. You can also see the ski trails on McCauley Mountain to the west.

Return by the same route.

Miles and Directions

0.0   Begin at the trailhead, following red NYSDEC markers into a hardwood forest.

0.2   Climb a length of slab, then turn left near the top of the slab to stay on the trail.

0.5   See your first view of the Fulton Chain of lakes.

0.6   Cross a short, wide bog bridge to another opening on the ledges.

1.0   FIRE TOWER! Return by the same route.

2.0   Arrive back at the trailhead.

20 Black Bear Mountain

A kid-friendly hike with a fun scramble up a rock chimney and a nice view of Seventh Lake from the summit.

Total distance: 4.0 miles
Type of hike: Out and back
Highest point: 2,454 feet
Vertical gain: 702 feet
Approximate hiking time: 3 hours

Canine compatibility: Not dog-friendly due to a 20-foot rock chimney
Map: USGS Eagle Bay Quad

Finding the trailhead: From the junction of Big Moose Road and NY 28 in Eagle Bay, take NY 28 east 1.1 miles toward Inlet. The trailhead and parking area are on the left (north) side of the road. Trailhead GPS: N43 45.848' / W74 47.632'

The Hike

Located in the Moose River Plains Wild Forest at the northeastern end of Fourth Lake, Black Bear Mountain is appropriately named. If you are observant, you will likely see bear tracks and scat in the clearings beside the lower trail, along with signs of deer and other wildlife. This hike is also appealing for the fun climb up the ledgy upper mountain and the view from the cliff at its summit.

Black Bear Mountain shares its trailhead and parking area with Rocky Mountain. The route up Black Bear Mountain leaves from the right (east) side of the parking lot, following the yellow NYSDEC markers. It crosses an old railroad bed, bending left (north) into the woods. It is a ski trail in the winter, and it is not open to motor vehicles.

From the sign-in box, the smooth path (a woods road) heads into the hardwood forest. At 0.2 mile, the woods road seems covered with cobblestones as it begins to climb gently. It becomes extra-broad with logs embedded in places to help stabilize the soil.

After passing a small clearing, the woods road narrows, becoming more like a footpath, but it widens again at the next small clearing. At 0.8 mile, just before reentering the woods, the trail comes to a fork. Bear right (east), heading uphill.

The route becomes a super-trail again. After passing another small clearing, it bends northeast, crossing some slab and becoming flat. Look for signs of deer and bear as you cross a muddy area.

At 1.0 mile, you cross a footbridge. Eventually, the woods road begins to climb again, heading east. There are more washed-out, eroded spots.

The road narrows to a footpath partway up the slope. After leveling off it continues to wind through the forest, then dips. At 1.6 miles, the path swings back to the east, ascending gently. An enormous conifer stands guard beside the trail on your left.

At 1.8 miles, you come to the junction with the trail from Seventh Lake. Continue straight, beginning the more aggressive part of the climb. The trail heads up through a jumble of rocks and roots following both blue and yellow markers. The summit looms ahead through the trees.

At 1.9 miles the path is blocked by a 20-foot rock chimney, which is more fun than challenging to climb. Above the ledge the trail angles south, climbing persistently, now following only blue markers. After more slab and ledge, a nice view to the southwest, mainly of nearby hills, opens up, then another view appears behind you of Fourth Lake.

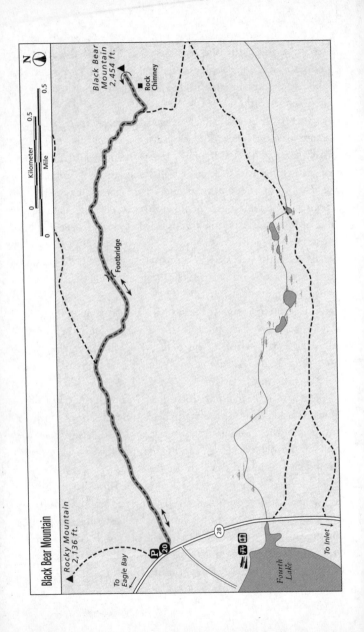

Black Bear Mountain

▲ Rocky Mountain
2,136 ft.

To Eagle Bay

P **20**

28

Fourth Lake

To Inlet

Footbridge

Black Bear Mountain
2,454 ft.

▲

■ Rock Chimney

N

0   0.5   Kilometer

0   0.5   Mile

The trail flattens over a length of slab, reaching the summit at 2.0 miles. The top of Black Bear Mountain is an elongated rock plateau with a nice view to the south of Seventh Lake, with Sixth Lake to the southwest beyond a hump of land. In the fall the summit area is ablaze with color from the maples and from the red berries and colorful leaves of the mountain ash.

Return by the same route.

Miles and Directions

0.0 Follow the broad path (woods road) into the hardwood forest.

0.2 Climb gently on a wide cobblestone-like path.

0.8 Bear right (east) at the fork, heading uphill.

1.0 Cross a footbridge.

1.6 Swing back to the east and ascend gently past an enormous conifer.

1.8 At the junction with the trail from Seventh Lake, continue straight, beginning the more aggressive part of the climb.

1.9 Climb a 20-foot rock chimney.

2.0 SUMMIT! Return by the same route.

4.0 Arrive back at the trailhead and parking area.

Eastern Region

T he Eastern Adirondacks include much more than the popular Lake George area. They encompass the entire eastern edge of the Adirondack Park, a long narrow swath from Ausable Chasm south along Lake Champlain to Fort Ticonderoga, then along NY 22 south to Whitehall on the Vermont border. From there, it zigzags west below the southern tip of Lake George, then continues back to Ausable Chasm along NY 9. While Lake George is certainly a focal point of the region, due mainly to its concentration of visitors, there are many acres of designated wilderness and wild forest with scenic mountaintops and pristine bodies of water to explore.

Because I-87 runs the length of the region parallel to NY 9, the trailheads in the Eastern Adirondacks are among the most accessible in the Park, yet these hikes deserve the same respect as more remote regions. Always wear appropriate clothing and footwear, and bring gear, food, and water for the backcountry. And don't forget the raingear and bug repellent!

21   Black Mountain

A nice, family hike to the highest mountain and some of the best views in the Lake George area.

Total distance: 5.2 miles
Type of hike: Out and back
Highest point: 2,650 feet
Vertical gain: 1,160 feet

Approximate hiking time: 4 hours
Canine compatibility:
Dog-friendly
Map: USGS Shelving Rock Quad

Finding the Trailhead: In Whitehall at the junction of NY 22 and US 4, go north on NY 22 for 7.0 miles. Turn left on CR 6 at the HULETTS LANDING sign. Go 2.7 miles, crossing into Lake George Park, then turn left on Pike Brook Road. The trailhead and parking lot are 0.8 mile farther on the right (west).

From Ticonderoga, take NY 22 south for 17.5 miles then turn right on CR 6. Trailhead GPS: N43 36.705' / W73 29.601'

The Hike

Black Mountain is the highest peak with a trail in the Lake George area. It crowns the eastern shore of the lake at its halfway point. There are two trails to its summit, one from the shore of the lake, requiring a boat, and the other one from Pike Brook Road, which is described here. This one is longer but climbs less vertically.

Unlike many of the prominent peaks in the Adirondack Park, Black Mountain is not named for a person. In the late 1800s a Professor J. Geugot from Princeton University dubbed the mountain "Black" because of its dark appearance due to the predominance of evergreens on its upper slopes.

From the trailhead, head up the old fire road, following the red NYSDEC markers and the orange snowmobile markers. Black Mountain is in the Lake George Wild Forest. In the Adirondacks, the difference between trails in a designated "wilderness" versus a "wild forest" is that horses, mountain bikes, and snowmobiles are allowed on trails in a wild forest. That said, horses and mountain bikes are not allowed on Black Mountain, and snowmobiles only share the flat approach to the peak.

At 0.2 mile, the fire road comes to a blocked road on your right. Follow the arrow and the FOOT TRAIL sign straight ahead to the west.

At 0.6 mile, bear right at another sign, avoiding a camp and a gate. The route is still level, though more eroded, with large cobblestone-like rocks underfoot. It seems more a wide footpath as you traverse through a mixed northern forest of beech, birch, and hemlock.

At 1.0 mile, the Lapland Pond Trail departs to your left (south). Continue straight (west) on the eroded road-like path, now crossing intermittent lengths of slab.

At 1.4 miles, the trail crosses a stream, which can get your feet wet during the springtime. It turns 90 degrees to the north, becoming even more eroded, as it begins to climb gently. A few minutes later it bends left (northwest) and climbs next to a seasonal stream, ascending more aggressively now.

At 2.1 miles, the ascent eases and the footing becomes smoother as you cross a mud hole. Grass grows along the slab. The climb is easier along this high plateau, but soon it tilts upward again, bending to the southwest after passing through a couple of switchbacks. There are still deciduous trees in the mix, though they are shrinking and getting thinner.

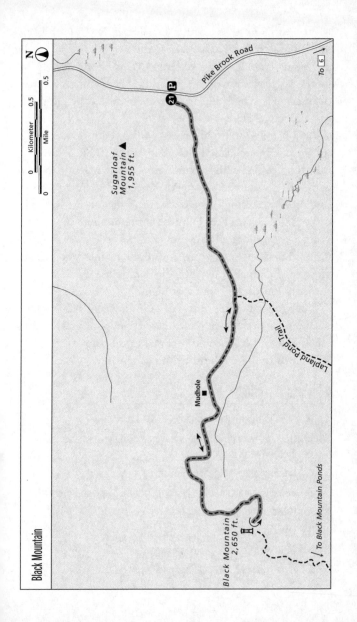

Black Mountain

N

Pike Brook Road

To 6

21 P

Sugarloaf
Mountain ▲
1,955 ft.

Mudhole

Lapland Pond Trail

Black Mountain
2,650 ft.

To Black Mountain Ponds

Kilometer   0.5

Mile   0.5

As you climb into a glade of tall hemlocks, look back for a glimpse of the High Peaks to the north. The trail levels off, passing among a lawn of ferns. It dips briefly, passing an impressive glacial erratic on your left. The footing becomes rocky again as you wind up the slope, eventually climbing over a ledge just below the boreal zone.

At 2.6 miles, the trail breaks out of the canopy onto a sizable rocky perch just below the summit. This is the best place for a picnic, with striking views of Lake George below to the north and the Green Mountains of Vermont to the east. Huletts Landing is the grassy peninsula on the east side of the lake. Sabbath Day Point is on the opposite shore. The footings of an old fire tower are here. The tower was manned until 1988 and was the only fire tower in the Adirondacks with a light on its cabin. Like a lighthouse in the sky, it warned pilots of the summit at night.

The true summit is marked with a cement block and a metal pipe above a search-and-rescue communication tower, which blocks the view and is closed to the public.

Return to the trailhead by the same route.

Miles and Directions

0.0   Start at the trailhead on Pike Brook Road.

0.2   Go straight, following the arrow and sign, ignoring the blocked road on your right.

0.6   Bear right at another sign, avoiding a camp and a gate.

1.0   Continue straight at the junction with the Lapland Pond Trail.

1.4   Cross a stream.

2.1   Cross a mud hole.

2.6   SUMMIT! Return by the same route.

5.2   Arrive back at the trailhead parking lot.

22 Poke-O-Moonshine

A short, steep hike along a nature trail to a fire tower atop a landmark 1,000-foot cliff with a fantastic view across Lake Champlain and into the Adirondack High Peaks.

Total distance: 2.2 miles
Type of hike: Out and back
Highest point: 2,180 feet
Vertical gain: 1,262 feet
Approximate hiking time: 2.5 hours

Canine compatibility: Dog-friendly. Do not allow dogs on the fire tower!
Map: USGS Clintonville Quad

Finding the Trailhead: From the junction of Deerhead Road (NY 14) and US 9 about 6.5 miles north of Lewis, head north on US 9 for 5.4 miles. The parking area and trailhead are at the former Poke-O-Moonshine campground on the left (west) side of the road. If approaching from Keeseville, at the junction of US 9 and NY 22, take US 9 south for 2.9 miles. Park at the campground, which is no longer in operation. Trailhead GPS: N44 24.202' / W73 30.148'

The Hike

Poke-O-Moonshine is an anglicized version of two Algonquin words, "pohqui," which means "broken," and "moosie," which means "smooth." It is an apt description of the well-used rock-strewn trail to the top of this famous cliff, a wall of granite gneiss that rises 1,000 feet from the valley floor. It is a popular spot for rock climbing, though some of the routes may be closed if peregrine falcons are nesting. Day hikers miss the vertical ascent up the cliff, but the trail feels almost as vertical. It's worth the short effort for the long 360-degree views from the fire tower on top.

From the toll booth at the entrance to the Poke-O-Moonshine Campground, turn left (southwest) down the grassy road that runs parallel to US 9. The road passes a number of former campsites before coming to the trailhead about 0.1 mile from the entrance to the campground.

At the trailhead, turn 90 degrees right (west) from the grass road in the campground and enter the woods following the red NYSDEC markers. The NYSDEC, Friends of Poke-O-Moonshine, and other volunteers turned this route to the top of mountain into an interpretive trail in 2000. Numbers on stakes along the trail point out various examples of natural history, geology, trail work, and flora. (Brochures are available at the sign-in box at the trailhead.)

The trail climbs steeply, passing several large glacial erratics. Whitewood asters bloom at the foot of maples, beech, and birches, the dominant trees in the forest mix. A number of stone water bars and other well-placed rocks help keep the trail in shape.

At 0.3 mile, the trail comes to a 40-foot rock wall. It bends left (south) along the base of the wall, still climbing. The footing becomes rockier as the path turns right over the top of the wall to a lookout. The view is mainly down I-87 except for one break in the far ridge, where you can see the Green Mountains in Vermont to the east.

The trail heads west, away from the cliff, and mellows on good footing. A few minutes later the climb resumes, and the trail becomes rougher, like a narrow, dry streambed. The footing improves again as you come alongside a streamlet, then it flattens as you cross a muddy area on stepping stones.

Ferns cover the ground to the left, and another huge boulder lies to your right.

At 0.7 mile, at the other end of the mud, the trail comes to the chimney and foundation of the old fire-watcher's cabin. Turn right (north) at the cabin remains, continuing uphill. The path soon flattens again, passing another lookout on your left, where you see Whiteface Mountain to the northwest and other High Peaks to the west.

The narrow trail is smooth and easygoing, basically along the edge of a cliff but with a row of trees as a buffer. Bunchberries bloom along the edges of the trail, signaling your elevation gain. Then, as you climb more steeply again, tall pines work their way into the forest mix and the canopy becomes more open.

At 0.9 mile, the trail bends right (southeast) and flattens one more time, almost doubling back on a high shoulder of the mountain. After passing through a grove of spindly striped maple and then climbing up a short bit of slab, the fire tower lies ahead at 1.1 miles.

The original fire tower atop Poke-O-Moonshine was built in 1912 with a wood cabin on top. The metal one that exists today was installed in 1916. It became a National Historic Landmark in 2001. It is not particularly high and the cabin is likely locked, but the view is terrific nonetheless. Lake Champlain takes up the entire eastern panorama, with Camel's Hump the dominant mountain beyond in the Green Mountains. The Adirondack High Peaks are equally spectacular to the northwest.

Return to the trailhead by the same route.

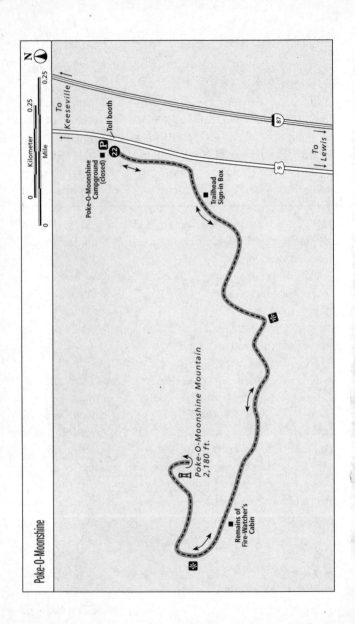

Poke-O-Moonshine

N

To
Keeseville

87

To
Lewis

9

Toll booth

P

22

Poke-O-Moonshine Campground
(Closed)

Trailhead
Sign-in Box

Poke-O-Moonshine Mountain
2,180 ft.

Remains of
Fire-Watcher's Cabin

Kilometer   0.25
Mile   0.25

About the Author

Born in Saranac Lake, New York, Lisa Densmore Ballard has been hiking, paddling, fishing, and skiing in the Adirondacks for most of her life. She spends her summers in the Adirondacks, visiting her family, spending time in the backcountry, and enjoy her second home on Chateaugay Lake.

A full-time freelance writer and photographer, Ballard's images have appeared in numerous publications including *Backpacker, Adirondack Life*, and *Adirondack Explorer*. She has an extensive stock-photo file of the Adirondacks. "If you can see it from a hiking trail, I've probably taken a picture of it," she says.

A past-president of the Outdoor Writers Association of America, Lisa complements her visual skills with writing. She has written hundreds of articles for as many magazines and websites, plus a number of books in addition to the first and second editions of this one: *Ski Faster! Guide to Ski Racing and High Performance Skiing, Best Hikes with Dogs: New Hampshire & Vermont, Hiking the Green Mountains, Hiking the White Mountains, Hiking the Adirondacks,* and *Backpacker Magazine's Predicting Weather: Predicting, Forecasting & Planning.*

To see Lisa's award-winning images and to learn more about her work, visit www.LisaDensmore.com.

Miles and Directions

0.0 Begin at the trailhead at the former Poke-O-Moonshine state campground, climbing up an interpretive trail.

0.3 Bear left at a 40-foot rock wall, climbing to the top of the wall for a view of the I-87 corridor.

0.7 Pass the remains of the old fire-watcher's cabin.

0.9 Double back on a high shoulder of the mountain.

1.1 FIRE TOWER! Return by the same route.

2.2 Arrive back at the trailhead on the edge of the former campground.